C-764   CAREER EXAMINATION SERIES

*This is your
PASSBOOK for...*

Steam Fitter's Helper

**Test Preparation Study Guide
Questions & Answers**

COPYRIGHT NOTICE

This book is SOLELY intended for, is sold ONLY to, and its use is RESTRICTED to individual, bona fide applicants or candidates who qualify by virtue of having seriously filed applications for appropriate license, certificate, professional and/or promotional advancement, higher school matriculation, scholarship, or other legitimate requirements of education and/or governmental authorities.

This book is NOT intended for use, class instruction, tutoring, training, duplication, copying, reprinting, excerption, or adaptation, etc., by:

1) Other publishers
2) Proprietors and/or Instructors of "Coaching" and/or Preparatory Courses
3) Personnel and/or Training Divisions of commercial, industrial, and governmental organizations
4) Schools, colleges, or universities and/or their departments and staffs, including teachers and other personnel
5) Testing Agencies or Bureaus
6) Study groups which seek by the purchase of a single volume to copy and/or duplicate and/or adapt this material for use by the group as a whole without having purchased individual volumes for each of the members of the group
7) Et al.

Such persons would be in violation of appropriate Federal and State statutes.

PROVISION OF LICENSING AGREEMENTS – Recognized educational, commercial, industrial, and governmental institutions and organizations, and others legitimately engaged in educational pursuits, including training, testing, and measurement activities, may address request for a licensing agreement to the copyright owners, who will determine whether, and under what conditions, including fees and charges, the materials in this book may be used them. In other words, a licensing facility exists for the legitimate use of the material in this book on other than an individual basis. However, it is asseverated and affirmed here that the material in this book CANNOT be used without the receipt of the express permission of such a licensing agreement from the Publishers. Inquiries re licensing should be addressed to the company, attention rights and permissions department.

All rights reserved, including the right of reproduction in whole or in part, in any form or by any means, electronic or mechanical, including photocopying, recording, or by any information storage and retrieval system, without permission in writing from the Publisher.

Copyright © 2025 by
National Learning Corporation

212 Michael Drive, Syosset, NY 11791
(516) 921-8888 • www.passbooks.com
E-mail: info@passbooks.com

PASSBOOK® SERIES

THE *PASSBOOK® SERIES* has been created to prepare applicants and candidates for the ultimate academic battlefield – the examination room.

At some time in our lives, each and every one of us may be required to take an examination – for validation, matriculation, admission, qualification, registration, certification, or licensure.

Based on the assumption that every applicant or candidate has met the basic formal educational standards, has taken the required number of courses, and read the necessary texts, the *PASSBOOK® SERIES* furnishes the one special preparation which may assure passing with confidence, instead of failing with insecurity. Examination questions – together with answers – are furnished as the basic vehicle for study so that the mysteries of the examination and its compounding difficulties may be eliminated or diminished by a sure method.

This book is meant to help you pass your examination provided that you qualify and are serious in your objective.

The entire field is reviewed through the huge store of content information which is succinctly presented through a provocative and challenging approach – the question-and-answer method.

A climate of success is established by furnishing the correct answers at the end of each test.

You soon learn to recognize types of questions, forms of questions, and patterns of questioning. You may even begin to anticipate expected outcomes.

You perceive that many questions are repeated or adapted so that you can gain acute insights, which may enable you to score many sure points.

You learn how to confront new questions, or types of questions, and to attack them confidently and work out the correct answers.

You note objectives and emphases, and recognize pitfalls and dangers, so that you may make positive educational adjustments.

Moreover, you are kept fully informed in relation to new concepts, methods, practices, and directions in the field.

You discover that you are actually taking the examination all the time: you are preparing for the examination by "taking" an examination, not by reading extraneous and/or supererogatory textbooks.

In short, this PASSBOOK®, used directedly, should be an important factor in helping you to pass your test.

STEAM FITTER'S HELPER

DUTIES AND RESPONSIBILITIES
Under direct supervision, assists in doing work relating to piping and equipment for compressed air and heating systems. Performs related work.

EXAMPLES OF TYPICAL TASKS
Assists in the installation, maintenance and repair of piping and equipment in air, steam and hot-water heating, air conditioning and processing systems. Assists in the installation of boilers, feedwater, vacuum and condensate equipment. Assists in the installation of fuel oil piping and related equipment. Assists in taking on-the-job measurements and laying out work from plans, specifications and/or sketches.

SCOPE OF THE EXAMINATION
The written test will be of the multiple-choice type and may include questions on heating, air conditioning and processing systems including piping, fittings, equipment and auxiliaries; inspection, maintenance and installation of systems and their components including measurement, selection and assembly of piping, fittings and equipment; tools, safety, proper housekeeping, shop arithmetic; comprehension of instructions and manuals and other related areas.

HOW TO TAKE A TEST

I. YOU MUST PASS AN EXAMINATION

A. *WHAT EVERY CANDIDATE SHOULD KNOW*

Examination applicants often ask us for help in preparing for the written test. What can I study in advance? What kinds of questions will be asked? How will the test be given? How will the papers be graded?

As an applicant for a civil service examination, you may be wondering about some of these things. Our purpose here is to suggest effective methods of advance study and to describe civil service examinations.

Your chances for success on this examination can be increased if you know how to prepare. Those "pre-examination jitters" can be reduced if you know what to expect. You can even experience an adventure in good citizenship if you know why civil service exams are given.

B. *WHY ARE CIVIL SERVICE EXAMINATIONS GIVEN?*

Civil service examinations are important to you in two ways. As a citizen, you want public jobs filled by employees who know how to do their work. As a job seeker, you want a fair chance to compete for that job on an equal footing with other candidates. The best-known means of accomplishing this two-fold goal is the competitive examination.

Exams are widely publicized throughout the nation. They may be administered for jobs in federal, state, city, municipal, town or village governments or agencies.

Any citizen may apply, with some limitations, such as the age or residence of applicants. Your experience and education may be reviewed to see whether you meet the requirements for the particular examination. When these requirements exist, they are reasonable and applied consistently to all applicants. Thus, a competitive examination may cause you some uneasiness now, but it is your privilege and safeguard.

C. *HOW ARE CIVIL SERVICE EXAMS DEVELOPED?*

Examinations are carefully written by trained technicians who are specialists in the field known as "psychological measurement," in consultation with recognized authorities in the field of work that the test will cover. These experts recommend the subject matter areas or skills to be tested; only those knowledges or skills important to your success on the job are included. The most reliable books and source materials available are used as references. Together, the experts and technicians judge the difficulty level of the questions.

Test technicians know how to phrase questions so that the problem is clearly stated. Their ethics do not permit "trick" or "catch" questions. Questions may have been tried out on sample groups, or subjected to statistical analysis, to determine their usefulness.

Written tests are often used in combination with performance tests, ratings of training and experience, and oral interviews. All of these measures combine to form the best-known means of finding the right person for the right job.

II. HOW TO PASS THE WRITTEN TEST

A. NATURE OF THE EXAMINATION

To prepare intelligently for civil service examinations, you should know how they differ from school examinations you have taken. In school you were assigned certain definite pages to read or subjects to cover. The examination questions were quite detailed and usually emphasized memory. Civil service exams, on the other hand, try to discover your present ability to perform the duties of a position, plus your potentiality to learn these duties. In other words, a civil service exam attempts to predict how successful you will be. Questions cover such a broad area that they cannot be as minute and detailed as school exam questions.

In the public service similar kinds of work, or positions, are grouped together in one "class." This process is known as *position-classification*. All the positions in a class are paid according to the salary range for that class. One class title covers all of these positions, and they are all tested by the same examination.

B. FOUR BASIC STEPS

1) Study the announcement

How, then, can you know what subjects to study? Our best answer is: "Learn as much as possible about the class of positions for which you've applied." The exam will test the knowledge, skills and abilities needed to do the work.

Your most valuable source of information about the position you want is the official exam announcement. This announcement lists the training and experience qualifications. Check these standards and apply only if you come reasonably close to meeting them.

The brief description of the position in the examination announcement offers some clues to the subjects which will be tested. Think about the job itself. Review the duties in your mind. Can you perform them, or are there some in which you are rusty? Fill in the blank spots in your preparation.

Many jurisdictions preview the written test in the exam announcement by including a section called "Knowledge and Abilities Required," "Scope of the Examination," or some similar heading. Here you will find out specifically what fields will be tested.

2) Review your own background

Once you learn in general what the position is all about, and what you need to know to do the work, ask yourself which subjects you already know fairly well and which need improvement. You may wonder whether to concentrate on improving your strong areas or on building some background in your fields of weakness. When the announcement has specified "some knowledge" or "considerable knowledge," or has used adjectives like "beginning principles of..." or "advanced ... methods," you can get a clue as to the number and difficulty of questions to be asked in any given field. More questions, and hence broader coverage, would be included for those subjects which are more important in the work. Now weigh your strengths and weaknesses against the job requirements and prepare accordingly.

3) Determine the level of the position

Another way to tell how intensively you should prepare is to understand the level of the job for which you are applying. Is it the entering level? In other words, is this the position in which beginners in a field of work are hired? Or is it an intermediate or advanced level? Sometimes this is indicated by such words as "Junior" or "Senior" in the class title. Other jurisdictions use Roman numerals to designate the level – Clerk I, Clerk II, for example. The word "Supervisor" sometimes appears in the title. If the level is not indicated by the title, check the description of duties. Will you be working under very close supervision, or will you have responsibility for independent decisions in this work?

4) Choose appropriate study materials

Now that you know the subjects to be examined and the relative amount of each subject to be covered, you can choose suitable study materials. For beginning level jobs, or even advanced ones, if you have a pronounced weakness in some aspect of your training, read a modern, standard textbook in that field. Be sure it is up to date and has general coverage. Such books are normally available at your library, and the librarian will be glad to help you locate one. For entry-level positions, questions of appropriate difficulty are chosen – neither highly advanced questions, nor those too simple. Such questions require careful thought but not advanced training.

If the position for which you are applying is technical or advanced, you will read more advanced, specialized material. If you are already familiar with the basic principles of your field, elementary textbooks would waste your time. Concentrate on advanced textbooks and technical periodicals. Think through the concepts and review difficult problems in your field.

These are all general sources. You can get more ideas on your own initiative, following these leads. For example, training manuals and publications of the government agency which employs workers in your field can be useful, particularly for technical and professional positions. A letter or visit to the government department involved may result in more specific study suggestions, and certainly will provide you with a more definite idea of the exact nature of the position you are seeking.

III. KINDS OF TESTS

Tests are used for purposes other than measuring knowledge and ability to perform specified duties. For some positions, it is equally important to test ability to make adjustments to new situations or to profit from training. In others, basic mental abilities not dependent on information are essential. Questions which test these things may not appear as pertinent to the duties of the position as those which test for knowledge and information. Yet they are often highly important parts of a fair examination. For very general questions, it is almost impossible to help you direct your study efforts. What we can do is to point out some of the more common of these general abilities needed in public service positions and describe some typical questions.

1) General information

Broad, general information has been found useful for predicting job success in some kinds of work. This is tested in a variety of ways, from vocabulary lists to questions about current events. Basic background in some field of work, such as sociology or economics, may be sampled in a group of questions. Often these are principles which have become familiar to most persons through exposure rather than through formal training. It is difficult to advise you how to study for these questions; being alert to the world around you is our best suggestion.

2) Verbal ability

An example of an ability needed in many positions is verbal or language ability. Verbal ability is, in brief, the ability to use and understand words. Vocabulary and grammar tests are typical measures of this ability. Reading comprehension or paragraph interpretation questions are common in many kinds of civil service tests. You are given a paragraph of written material and asked to find its central meaning.

3) Numerical ability

Number skills can be tested by the familiar arithmetic problem, by checking paired lists of numbers to see which are alike and which are different, or by interpreting charts and graphs. In the latter test, a graph may be printed in the test booklet which you are asked to use as the basis for answering questions.

4) Observation

A popular test for law-enforcement positions is the observation test. A picture is shown to you for several minutes, then taken away. Questions about the picture test your ability to observe both details and larger elements.

5) Following directions

In many positions in the public service, the employee must be able to carry out written instructions dependably and accurately. You may be given a chart with several columns, each column listing a variety of information. The questions require you to carry out directions involving the information given in the chart.

6) Skills and aptitudes

Performance tests effectively measure some manual skills and aptitudes. When the skill is one in which you are trained, such as typing or shorthand, you can practice. These tests are often very much like those given in business school or high school courses. For many of the other skills and aptitudes, however, no short-time preparation can be made. Skills and abilities natural to you or that you have developed throughout your lifetime are being tested.

Many of the general questions just described provide all the data needed to answer the questions and ask you to use your reasoning ability to find the answers. Your best preparation for these tests, as well as for tests of facts and ideas, is to be at your physical and mental best. You, no doubt, have your own methods of getting into an exam-taking mood and keeping "in shape." The next section lists some ideas on this subject.

IV. KINDS OF QUESTIONS

Only rarely is the "essay" question, which you answer in narrative form, used in civil service tests. Civil service tests are usually of the short-answer type. Full instructions for answering these questions will be given to you at the examination. But in case this is your first experience with short-answer questions and separate answer sheets, here is what you need to know:

1) Multiple-choice Questions

Most popular of the short-answer questions is the "multiple choice" or "best answer" question. It can be used, for example, to test for factual knowledge, ability to solve problems or judgment in meeting situations found at work.

A multiple-choice question is normally one of three types—
- It can begin with an incomplete statement followed by several possible endings. You are to find the one ending which *best* completes the statement, although some of the others may not be entirely wrong.
- It can also be a complete statement in the form of a question which is answered by choosing one of the statements listed.

- It can be in the form of a problem – again you select the best answer.

Here is an example of a multiple-choice question with a discussion which should give you some clues as to the method for choosing the right answer:

When an employee has a complaint about his assignment, the action which will *best* help him overcome his difficulty is to
   A. discuss his difficulty with his coworkers
   B. take the problem to the head of the organization
   C. take the problem to the person who gave him the assignment
   D. say nothing to anyone about his complaint

In answering this question, you should study each of the choices to find which is best. Consider choice "A" – Certainly an employee may discuss his complaint with fellow employees, but no change or improvement can result, and the complaint remains unresolved. Choice "B" is a poor choice since the head of the organization probably does not know what assignment you have been given, and taking your problem to him is known as "going over the head" of the supervisor. The supervisor, or person who made the assignment, is the person who can clarify it or correct any injustice. Choice "C" is, therefore, correct. To say nothing, as in choice "D," is unwise. Supervisors have and interest in knowing the problems employees are facing, and the employee is seeking a solution to his problem.

2) True/False Questions

The "true/false" or "right/wrong" form of question is sometimes used. Here a complete statement is given. Your job is to decide whether the statement is right or wrong.

SAMPLE: A roaming cell-phone call to a nearby city costs less than a non-roaming call to a distant city.

This statement is wrong, or false, since roaming calls are more expensive.
This is not a complete list of all possible question forms, although most of the others are variations of these common types. You will always get complete directions for answering questions. Be sure you understand *how* to mark your answers – ask questions until you do.

V. RECORDING YOUR ANSWERS

Computer terminals are used more and more today for many different kinds of exams.
For an examination with very few applicants, you may be told to record your answers in the test booklet itself. Separate answer sheets are much more common. If this separate answer sheet is to be scored by machine – and this is often the case – it is highly important that you mark your answers correctly in order to get credit.
An electronic scoring machine is often used in civil service offices because of the speed with which papers can be scored. Machine-scored answer sheets must be marked with a pencil, which will be given to you. This pencil has a high graphite content which responds to the electronic scoring machine. As a matter of fact, stray dots may register as answers, so do not let your pencil rest on the answer sheet while you are pondering the correct answer. Also, if your pencil lead breaks or is otherwise defective, ask for another.

Since the answer sheet will be dropped in a slot in the scoring machine, be careful not to bend the corners or get the paper crumpled.

The answer sheet normally has five vertical columns of numbers, with 30 numbers to a column. These numbers correspond to the question numbers in your test booklet. After each number, going across the page are four or five pairs of dotted lines. These short dotted lines have small letters or numbers above them. The first two pairs may also have a "T" or "F" above the letters. This indicates that the first two pairs only are to be used if the questions are of the true-false type. If the questions are multiple choice, disregard the "T" and "F" and pay attention only to the small letters or numbers.

Answer your questions in the manner of the sample that follows:

32. The largest city in the United States is
 A. Washington, D.C.
 B. New York City
 C. Chicago
 D. Detroit
 E. San Francisco

1) Choose the answer you think is best. (New York City is the largest, so "B" is correct.)
2) Find the row of dotted lines numbered the same as the question you are answering. (Find row number 32)
3) Find the pair of dotted lines corresponding to the answer. (Find the pair of lines under the mark "B.")
4) Make a solid black mark between the dotted lines.

VI. BEFORE THE TEST

Common sense will help you find procedures to follow to get ready for an examination. Too many of us, however, overlook these sensible measures. Indeed, nervousness and fatigue have been found to be the most serious reasons why applicants fail to do their best on civil service tests. Here is a list of reminders:

- Begin your preparation early – Don't wait until the last minute to go scurrying around for books and materials or to find out what the position is all about.
- Prepare continuously – An hour a night for a week is better than an all-night cram session. This has been definitely established. What is more, a night a week for a month will return better dividends than crowding your study into a shorter period of time.
- Locate the place of the exam – You have been sent a notice telling you when and where to report for the examination. If the location is in a different town or otherwise unfamiliar to you, it would be well to inquire the best route and learn something about the building.
- Relax the night before the test – Allow your mind to rest. Do not study at all that night. Plan some mild recreation or diversion; then go to bed early and get a good night's sleep.
- Get up early enough to make a leisurely trip to the place for the test – This way unforeseen events, traffic snarls, unfamiliar buildings, etc. will not upset you.
- Dress comfortably – A written test is not a fashion show. You will be known by number and not by name, so wear something comfortable.

- Leave excess paraphernalia at home – Shopping bags and odd bundles will get in your way. You need bring only the items mentioned in the official notice you received; usually everything you need is provided. Do not bring reference books to the exam. They will only confuse those last minutes and be taken away from you when in the test room.
- Arrive somewhat ahead of time – If because of transportation schedules you must get there very early, bring a newspaper or magazine to take your mind off yourself while waiting.
- Locate the examination room – When you have found the proper room, you will be directed to the seat or part of the room where you will sit. Sometimes you are given a sheet of instructions to read while you are waiting. Do not fill out any forms until you are told to do so; just read them and be prepared.
- Relax and prepare to listen to the instructions
- If you have any physical problem that may keep you from doing your best, be sure to tell the test administrator. If you are sick or in poor health, you really cannot do your best on the exam. You can come back and take the test some other time.

VII. AT THE TEST

The day of the test is here and you have the test booklet in your hand. The temptation to get going is very strong. Caution! There is more to success than knowing the right answers. You must know how to identify your papers and understand variations in the type of short-answer question used in this particular examination. Follow these suggestions for maximum results from your efforts:

1) Cooperate with the monitor

The test administrator has a duty to create a situation in which you can be as much at ease as possible. He will give instructions, tell you when to begin, check to see that you are marking your answer sheet correctly, and so on. He is not there to guard you, although he will see that your competitors do not take unfair advantage. He wants to help you do your best.

2) Listen to all instructions

Don't jump the gun! Wait until you understand all directions. In most civil service tests you get more time than you need to answer the questions. So don't be in a hurry. Read each word of instructions until you clearly understand the meaning. Study the examples, listen to all announcements and follow directions. Ask questions if you do not understand what to do.

3) Identify your papers

Civil service exams are usually identified by number only. You will be assigned a number; you must not put your name on your test papers. Be sure to copy your number correctly. Since more than one exam may be given, copy your exact examination title.

4) Plan your time

Unless you are told that a test is a "speed" or "rate of work" test, speed itself is usually not important. Time enough to answer all the questions will be provided, but this does not mean that you have all day. An overall time limit has been set. Divide the total time (in minutes) by the number of questions to determine the approximate time you have for each question.

5) Do not linger over difficult questions

If you come across a difficult question, mark it with a paper clip (useful to have along) and come back to it when you have been through the booklet. One caution if you do this – be sure to skip a number on your answer sheet as well. Check often to be sure that you have not lost your place and that you are marking in the row numbered the same as the question you are answering.

6) Read the questions

Be sure you know what the question asks! Many capable people are unsuccessful because they failed to *read* the questions correctly.

7) Answer all questions

Unless you have been instructed that a penalty will be deducted for incorrect answers, it is better to guess than to omit a question.

8) Speed tests

It is often better NOT to guess on speed tests. It has been found that on timed tests people are tempted to spend the last few seconds before time is called in marking answers at random – without even reading them – in the hope of picking up a few extra points. To discourage this practice, the instructions may warn you that your score will be "corrected" for guessing. That is, a penalty will be applied. The incorrect answers will be deducted from the correct ones, or some other penalty formula will be used.

9) Review your answers

If you finish before time is called, go back to the questions you guessed or omitted to give them further thought. Review other answers if you have time.

10) Return your test materials

If you are ready to leave before others have finished or time is called, take ALL your materials to the monitor and leave quietly. Never take any test material with you. The monitor can discover whose papers are not complete, and taking a test booklet may be grounds for disqualification.

VIII. EXAMINATION TECHNIQUES

1) Read the general instructions carefully. These are usually printed on the first page of the exam booklet. As a rule, these instructions refer to the timing of the examination; the fact that you should not start work until the signal and must stop work at a signal, etc. If there are any *special* instructions, such as a choice of questions to be answered, make sure that you note this instruction carefully.

2) When you are ready to start work on the examination, that is as soon as the signal has been given, read the instructions to each question booklet, underline any key words or phrases, such as *least, best, outline, describe* and the like. In this way you will tend to answer as requested rather than discover on reviewing your paper that you *listed without describing*, that you selected the *worst* choice rather than the *best* choice, etc.

3) If the examination is of the objective or multiple-choice type – that is, each question will also give a series of possible answers: A, B, C or D, and you are called upon to select the best answer and write the letter next to that answer on your answer paper – it is advisable to start answering each question in turn. There may be anywhere from 50 to 100 such questions in the three or four hours allotted and you can see how much time would be taken if you read through all the questions before beginning to answer any. Furthermore, if you come across a question or group of questions which you know would be difficult to answer, it would undoubtedly affect your handling of all the other questions.

4) If the examination is of the essay type and contains but a few questions, it is a moot point as to whether you should read all the questions before starting to answer any one. Of course, if you are given a choice – say five out of seven and the like – then it is essential to read all the questions so you can eliminate the two that are most difficult. If, however, you are asked to answer all the questions, there may be danger in trying to answer the easiest one first because you may find that you will spend too much time on it. The best technique is to answer the first question, then proceed to the second, etc.

5) Time your answers. Before the exam begins, write down the time it started, then add the time allowed for the examination and write down the time it must be completed, then divide the time available somewhat as follows:
   - If 3-1/2 hours are allowed, that would be 210 minutes. If you have 80 objective-type questions, that would be an average of 2-1/2 minutes per question. Allow yourself no more than 2 minutes per question, or a total of 160 minutes, which will permit about 50 minutes to review.
   - If for the time allotment of 210 minutes there are 7 essay questions to answer, that would average about 30 minutes a question. Give yourself only 25 minutes per question so that you have about 35 minutes to review.

6) The most important instruction is to *read each question* and make sure you know what is wanted. The second most important instruction is to *time yourself properly* so that you answer every question. The third most important instruction is to *answer every question*. Guess if you have to but include something for each question. Remember that you will receive no credit for a blank and will probably receive some credit if you write something in answer to an essay question. If you guess a letter – say "B" for a multiple-choice question – you may have guessed right. If you leave a blank as an answer to a multiple-choice question, the examiners may respect your feelings but it will not add a point to your score. Some exams may penalize you for wrong answers, so in such cases *only*, you may not want to guess unless you have some basis for your answer.

7) Suggestions
   a. Objective-type questions
      1. Examine the question booklet for proper sequence of pages and questions
      2. Read all instructions carefully
      3. Skip any question which seems too difficult; return to it after all other questions have been answered
      4. Apportion your time properly; do not spend too much time on any single question or group of questions

5. Note and underline key words – *all, most, fewest, least, best, worst, same, opposite,* etc.
6. Pay particular attention to negatives
7. Note unusual option, e.g., unduly long, short, complex, different or similar in content to the body of the question
8. Observe the use of "hedging" words – *probably, may, most likely,* etc.
9. Make sure that your answer is put next to the same number as the question
10. Do not second-guess unless you have good reason to believe the second answer is definitely more correct
11. Cross out original answer if you decide another answer is more accurate; do not erase until you are ready to hand your paper in
12. Answer all questions; guess unless instructed otherwise
13. Leave time for review

  b. Essay questions
    1. Read each question carefully
    2. Determine exactly what is wanted. Underline key words or phrases.
    3. Decide on outline or paragraph answer
    4. Include many different points and elements unless asked to develop any one or two points or elements
    5. Show impartiality by giving pros and cons unless directed to select one side only
    6. Make and write down any assumptions you find necessary to answer the questions
    7. Watch your English, grammar, punctuation and choice of words
    8. Time your answers; don't crowd material

8) Answering the essay question

Most essay questions can be answered by framing the specific response around several key words or ideas. Here are a few such key words or ideas:

M's: manpower, materials, methods, money, management
P's: purpose, program, policy, plan, procedure, practice, problems, pitfalls, personnel, public relations

  a. Six basic steps in handling problems:
    1. Preliminary plan and background development
    2. Collect information, data and facts
    3. Analyze and interpret information, data and facts
    4. Analyze and develop solutions as well as make recommendations
    5. Prepare report and sell recommendations
    6. Install recommendations and follow up effectiveness

  b. Pitfalls to avoid
    1. *Taking things for granted* – A statement of the situation does not necessarily imply that each of the elements is necessarily true; for example, a complaint may be invalid and biased so that all that can be taken for granted is that a complaint has been registered

2. *Considering only one side of a situation* – Wherever possible, indicate several alternatives and then point out the reasons you selected the best one
3. *Failing to indicate follow up* – Whenever your answer indicates action on your part, make certain that you will take proper follow-up action to see how successful your recommendations, procedures or actions turn out to be
4. *Taking too long in answering any single question* – Remember to time your answers properly

IX. AFTER THE TEST

Scoring procedures differ in detail among civil service jurisdictions although the general principles are the same. Whether the papers are hand-scored or graded by machine we have described, they are nearly always graded by number. That is, the person who marks the paper knows only the number – never the name – of the applicant. Not until all the papers have been graded will they be matched with names. If other tests, such as training and experience or oral interview ratings have been given, scores will be combined. Different parts of the examination usually have different weights. For example, the written test might count 60 percent of the final grade, and a rating of training and experience 40 percent. In many jurisdictions, veterans will have a certain number of points added to their grades.

After the final grade has been determined, the names are placed in grade order and an eligible list is established. There are various methods for resolving ties between those who get the same final grade – probably the most common is to place first the name of the person whose application was received first. Job offers are made from the eligible list in the order the names appear on it. You will be notified of your grade and your rank as soon as all these computations have been made. This will be done as rapidly as possible.

People who are found to meet the requirements in the announcement are called "eligibles." Their names are put on a list of eligible candidates. An eligible's chances of getting a job depend on how high he stands on this list and how fast agencies are filling jobs from the list.

When a job is to be filled from a list of eligibles, the agency asks for the names of people on the list of eligibles for that job. When the civil service commission receives this request, it sends to the agency the names of the three people highest on this list. Or, if the job to be filled has specialized requirements, the office sends the agency the names of the top three persons who meet these requirements from the general list.

The appointing officer makes a choice from among the three people whose names were sent to him. If the selected person accepts the appointment, the names of the others are put back on the list to be considered for future openings.

That is the rule in hiring from all kinds of eligible lists, whether they are for typist, carpenter, chemist, or something else. For every vacancy, the appointing officer has his choice of any one of the top three eligibles on the list. This explains why the person whose name is on top of the list sometimes does not get an appointment when some of the persons lower on the list do. If the appointing officer chooses the second or third eligible, the No. 1 eligible does not get a job at once, but stays on the list until he is appointed or the list is terminated.

X. HOW TO PASS THE INTERVIEW TEST

The examination for which you applied requires an oral interview test. You have already taken the written test and you are now being called for the interview test – the final part of the formal examination.

You may think that it is not possible to prepare for an interview test and that there are no procedures to follow during an interview. Our purpose is to point out some things you can do in advance that will help you and some good rules to follow and pitfalls to avoid while you are being interviewed.

What is an interview supposed to test?

The written examination is designed to test the technical knowledge and competence of the candidate; the oral is designed to evaluate intangible qualities, not readily measured otherwise, and to establish a list showing the relative fitness of each candidate – as measured against his competitors – for the position sought. Scoring is not on the basis of "right" and "wrong," but on a sliding scale of values ranging from "not passable" to "outstanding." As a matter of fact, it is possible to achieve a relatively low score without a single "incorrect" answer because of evident weakness in the qualities being measured.

Occasionally, an examination may consist entirely of an oral test – either an individual or a group oral. In such cases, information is sought concerning the technical knowledges and abilities of the candidate, since there has been no written examination for this purpose. More commonly, however, an oral test is used to supplement a written examination.

Who conducts interviews?

The composition of oral boards varies among different jurisdictions. In nearly all, a representative of the personnel department serves as chairman. One of the members of the board may be a representative of the department in which the candidate would work. In some cases, "outside experts" are used, and, frequently, a businessman or some other representative of the general public is asked to serve. Labor and management or other special groups may be represented. The aim is to secure the services of experts in the appropriate field.

However the board is composed, it is a good idea (and not at all improper or unethical) to ascertain in advance of the interview who the members are and what groups they represent. When you are introduced to them, you will have some idea of their backgrounds and interests, and at least you will not stutter and stammer over their names.

What should be done before the interview?

While knowledge about the board members is useful and takes some of the surprise element out of the interview, there is other preparation which is more substantive. It *is* possible to prepare for an oral interview – in several ways:

1) Keep a copy of your application and review it carefully before the interview

This may be the only document before the oral board, and the starting point of the interview. Know what education and experience you have listed there, and the sequence and dates of all of it. Sometimes the board will ask you to review the highlights of your experience for them; you should not have to hem and haw doing it.

2) Study the class specification and the examination announcement

Usually, the oral board has one or both of these to guide them. The qualities, characteristics or knowledges required by the position sought are stated in these documents. They offer valuable clues as to the nature of the oral interview. For example, if the job involves supervisory responsibilities, the announcement will usually indicate that knowledge of modern supervisory methods and the qualifications of the candidate as a supervisor will be tested. If so, you can expect such questions, frequently in the form of a hypothetical situation which you are expected to solve. NEVER go into an oral without knowledge of the duties and responsibilities of the job you seek.

3) Think through each qualification required

Try to visualize the kind of questions you would ask if you were a board member. How well could you answer them? Try especially to appraise your own knowledge and background in each area, *measured against the job sought*, and identify any areas in which you are weak. Be critical and realistic – do not flatter yourself.

4) Do some general reading in areas in which you feel you may be weak

For example, if the job involves supervision and your past experience has NOT, some general reading in supervisory methods and practices, particularly in the field of human relations, might be useful. Do NOT study agency procedures or detailed manuals. The oral board will be testing your understanding and capacity, not your memory.

5) Get a good night's sleep and watch your general health and mental attitude

You will want a clear head at the interview. Take care of a cold or any other minor ailment, and of course, no hangovers.

What should be done on the day of the interview?

Now comes the day of the interview itself. Give yourself plenty of time to get there. Plan to arrive somewhat ahead of the scheduled time, particularly if your appointment is in the fore part of the day. If a previous candidate fails to appear, the board might be ready for you a bit early. By early afternoon an oral board is almost invariably behind schedule if there are many candidates, and you may have to wait. Take along a book or magazine to read, or your application to review, but leave any extraneous material in the waiting room when you go in for your interview. In any event, relax and compose yourself.

The matter of dress is important. The board is forming impressions about you – from your experience, your manners, your attitude, and your appearance. Give your personal appearance careful attention. Dress your best, but not your flashiest. Choose conservative, appropriate clothing, and be sure it is immaculate. This is a business interview, and your appearance should indicate that you regard it as such. Besides, being well groomed and properly dressed will help boost your confidence.

Sooner or later, someone will call your name and escort you into the interview room. *This is it.* From here on you are on your own. It is too late for any more preparation. But remember, you asked for this opportunity to prove your fitness, and you are here because your request was granted.

What happens when you go in?

The usual sequence of events will be as follows: The clerk (who is often the board stenographer) will introduce you to the chairman of the oral board, who will introduce you to the other members of the board. Acknowledge the introductions before you sit down. Do not be surprised if you find a microphone facing you or a stenotypist sitting by. Oral interviews are usually recorded in the event of an appeal or other review.

Usually the chairman of the board will open the interview by reviewing the highlights of your education and work experience from your application – primarily for the benefit of the other members of the board, as well as to get the material into the record. Do not interrupt or comment unless there is an error or significant misinterpretation; if that is the case, do not hesitate. But do not quibble about insignificant matters. Also, he will usually ask you some question about your education, experience or your present job – partly to get you to start talking and to establish the interviewing "rapport." He may start the actual questioning, or turn it over to one of the other members. Frequently, each member undertakes the questioning on a particular area, one in which he is perhaps most competent, so you can expect each member to participate in the examination. Because time is limited, you may also expect some rather abrupt switches in the direction the questioning takes, so do not be upset by it. Normally, a board member will not pursue a single line of questioning unless he discovers a particular strength or weakness.

After each member has participated, the chairman will usually ask whether any member has any further questions, then will ask you if you have anything you wish to add. Unless you are expecting this question, it may floor you. Worse, it may start you off on an extended, extemporaneous speech. The board is not usually seeking more information. The question is principally to offer you a last opportunity to present further qualifications or to indicate that you have nothing to add. So, if you feel that a significant qualification or characteristic has been overlooked, it is proper to point it out in a sentence or so. Do not compliment the board on the thoroughness of their examination – they have been sketchy, and you know it. If you wish, merely say, "No thank you, I have nothing further to add." This is a point where you can "talk yourself out" of a good impression or fail to present an important bit of information. Remember, *you close the interview yourself.*

The chairman will then say, "That is all, Mr. _____, thank you." Do not be startled; the interview is over, and quicker than you think. Thank him, gather your belongings and take your leave. Save your sigh of relief for the other side of the door.

How to put your best foot forward

Throughout this entire process, you may feel that the board individually and collectively is trying to pierce your defenses, seek out your hidden weaknesses and embarrass and confuse you. Actually, this is not true. They are obliged to make an appraisal of your qualifications for the job you are seeking, and they want to see you in your best light. Remember, they must interview all candidates and a non-cooperative candidate may become a failure in spite of their best efforts to bring out his qualifications. Here are 15 suggestions that will help you:

1) Be natural – Keep your attitude confident, not cocky

If you are not confident that you can do the job, do not expect the board to be. Do not apologize for your weaknesses, try to bring out your strong points. The board is interested in a positive, not negative, presentation. Cockiness will antagonize any board member and make him wonder if you are covering up a weakness by a false show of strength.

2) Get comfortable, but don't lounge or sprawl

Sit erectly but not stiffly. A careless posture may lead the board to conclude that you are careless in other things, or at least that you are not impressed by the importance of the occasion. Either conclusion is natural, even if incorrect. Do not fuss with your clothing, a pencil or an ashtray. Your hands may occasionally be useful to emphasize a point; do not let them become a point of distraction.

3) Do not wisecrack or make small talk

This is a serious situation, and your attitude should show that you consider it as such. Further, the time of the board is limited – they do not want to waste it, and neither should you.

4) Do not exaggerate your experience or abilities

In the first place, from information in the application or other interviews and sources, the board may know more about you than you think. Secondly, you probably will not get away with it. An experienced board is rather adept at spotting such a situation, so do not take the chance.

5) If you know a board member, do not make a point of it, yet do not hide it

Certainly you are not fooling him, and probably not the other members of the board. Do not try to take advantage of your acquaintanceship – it will probably do you little good.

6) Do not dominate the interview

Let the board do that. They will give you the clues – do not assume that you have to do all the talking. Realize that the board has a number of questions to ask you, and do not try to take up all the interview time by showing off your extensive knowledge of the answer to the first one.

7) Be attentive

You only have 20 minutes or so, and you should keep your attention at its sharpest throughout. When a member is addressing a problem or question to you, give him your undivided attention. Address your reply principally to him, but do not exclude the other board members.

8) Do not interrupt

A board member may be stating a problem for you to analyze. He will ask you a question when the time comes. Let him state the problem, and wait for the question.

9) Make sure you understand the question

Do not try to answer until you are sure what the question is. If it is not clear, restate it in your own words or ask the board member to clarify it for you. However, do not haggle about minor elements.

10) Reply promptly but not hastily

A common entry on oral board rating sheets is "candidate responded readily," or "candidate hesitated in replies." Respond as promptly and quickly as you can, but do not jump to a hasty, ill-considered answer.

11) Do not be peremptory in your answers

A brief answer is proper – but do not fire your answer back. That is a losing game from your point of view. The board member can probably ask questions much faster than you can answer them.

12) Do not try to create the answer you think the board member wants

He is interested in what kind of mind you have and how it works – not in playing games. Furthermore, he can usually spot this practice and will actually grade you down on it.

13) Do not switch sides in your reply merely to agree with a board member

Frequently, a member will take a contrary position merely to draw you out and to see if you are willing and able to defend your point of view. Do not start a debate, yet do not surrender a good position. If a position is worth taking, it is worth defending.

14) Do not be afraid to admit an error in judgment if you are shown to be wrong

The board knows that you are forced to reply without any opportunity for careful consideration. Your answer may be demonstrably wrong. If so, admit it and get on with the interview.

15) Do not dwell at length on your present job

The opening question may relate to your present assignment. Answer the question but do not go into an extended discussion. You are being examined for a *new* job, not your present one. As a matter of fact, try to phrase ALL your answers in terms of the job for which you are being examined.

Basis of Rating

Probably you will forget most of these "do's" and "don'ts" when you walk into the oral interview room. Even remembering them all will not ensure you a passing grade. Perhaps you did not have the qualifications in the first place. But remembering them will help you to put your best foot forward, without treading on the toes of the board members.

Rumor and popular opinion to the contrary notwithstanding, an oral board wants you to make the best appearance possible. They know you are under pressure – but they also want to see how you respond to it as a guide to what your reaction would be under the pressures of the job you seek. They will be influenced by the degree of poise you display, the personal traits you show and the manner in which you respond.

ABOUT THIS BOOK

This book contains tests divided into Examination Sections. Go through each test, answering every question in the margin. We have also attached a sample answer sheet at the back of the book that can be removed and used. At the end of each test look at the answer key and check your answers. On the ones you got wrong, look at the right answer choice and learn. Do not fill in the answers first. Do not memorize the questions and answers, but understand the answer and principles involved. On your test, the questions will likely be different from the samples. Questions are changed and new ones added. If you understand these past questions you should have success with any changes that arise. Tests may consist of several types of questions. We have additional books on each subject should more study be advisable or necessary for you. Finally, the more you study, the better prepared you will be. This book is intended to be the last thing you study before you walk into the examination room. Prior study of relevant texts is also recommended. NLC publishes some of these in our Fundamental Series. Knowledge and good sense are important factors in passing your exam. Good luck also helps. So now study this Passbook, absorb the material contained within and take that knowledge into the examination. Then do your best to pass that exam.

EXAMINATION SECTION

EXAMINATION SECTION
TEST 1

DIRECTIONS: Each question or incomplete statement is followed by several suggested answers or completions. Select the one that BEST answers the question or completes the statement. *PRINT THE LETTER OF THE CORRECT ANSWER IN THE SPACE AT THE RIGHT.*

1. Of the following, the foil which contains all the tools necessary to properly install a screwed fitting into an existing continuous steam main is

    A. hacksaw, ratchet wrench die, stillson wrench, rule
    B. ratchet wrench die, cold chisel, hammer, rule
    C. pipe vise, pipe reamer, pipe cutter, rule, and hacksaw
    D. center punch, pipe cutter, reamer, pipe die, and stock

    1.____

2. The MINIMUM diameter of pipe that may be used for gas piping in the city is

    A. 3/4" B. 5/8" C. 1/2" D. 3/8"

    2.____

3. A tee fitting that has the branch larger than the run is GENERALLY called a _____ tee.

    A. branch   B. bull head
    C. drop   D. double sweep

    3.____

4. The proper type of fitting to use in a horizontal hot water heating main, when changing pipe size, is generally known as a(n)

    A. hexagon bushing   B. face bushing
    C. concentric reducer   D. eccentric reducer

    4.____

5. Pitch elbows are elbbws having

    A. built-in drain plugs
    B. under-size threads
    C. one end threaded and the other caulked
    D. special provisions for drainage

    5.____

6. Of the following types of pipe material, the one which will expand the LEAST when heated is

    A. steel   B. wrought iron
    C. cast iron   D. brass

    6.____

7. By which series of dimensions is the cross-fitting shown at the right BEST described?
    A. 2 1/2 x 1 1/4 x 2 1/4 x 1 1/2
    B. 2 1/2 x 2 1/4 x 1 1/4 x 1 1/2
    C. 2 1/2 x 1 1/2 x 2 1/4 x 1 1/4
    D. 2 1/2 x 2 1/4 x 1 1/2 x 1 1/4

    7.____

8. If the circumference of a circle is equal to 31.416 inches, then its diameter, in inches, is equal to MOST NEARLY

   A. 8   B. 9   C. 10   D. 13

9. Fittings in a fire standpipe system in the city MUST be made of

   A. brass
   B. lead
   C. monel
   D. malleable cast iron

10. If the outside diameter of a pipe is 14 inches and the wall thickness is 1/2 inch, then the inside area of the pipe, in square inches, is MOST NEARLY

    A. 125   B. 133   C. 143   D. 154

11. Pipe having a schedule number of 40 corresponds MOST NEARLY to _____ pipe.

    A. standard
    B. extra strong
    C. double extra strong
    D. type M copper

12. For which one of the following temperature ranges should a steam fitter use a valve that is designated as 125 OWC?

    A. 30-100° F   B. 125-175° F   C. 180-200° F   D. 212-250° F

13. A *packed expansion joint* is USUALLY installed on a _____ line.

    A. high pressure water
    B. medium pressure steam
    C. compressed air
    D. condensate

14. Of the following types of pipe, the one that is USUALLY used for general plant applications in the low and medium steam pressure range is

    A. alloy-steel
    B. monel
    C. brass
    D. wrought iron

15. With reference to making up steam lines, flange fittings are GENERALLY used for pipe diameters of NOT LESS THAN

    A. 1"   B. 2"   C. 3"   D. 4"

16. Of the following kinds of wedges used in gate valves, the one that is MOST generally used for steam service is the _____ type.

    A. solid
    B. double disc-taper seat
    C. double disc-parallel seat
    D. split

17. Of the following valve trim symbols, the one which designates a valve trim made of monel material is

    A. MI   B. SM   C. NI CU   D. 8-18

18. Of the following devices used in steam heating systems, the one that is NOT used to trap or hold steam is the _____ trap.

    A. float
    B. thermostatic
    C. inverted bucket
    D. boiler return

19. The type of gasket material that is GENERALLY used between pipe flanges on a super-heated steam line is

    A. asbestos
    B. cotton impregnated with graphite
    C. rubber
    D. monel and copper

20. The recommended depth of dirt pockets used on steam heating systems (not including unit heaters) having thermostatic traps is USUALLY _____ deep.

    A. 1"   B. 4"   C. 6"   D. 10"

21. Of the following types of valves, the one which is generally used where extremely close regulation of flow is required is the _____ valve.

    A. needle   B. gate   C. globe   D. blow-off

22. In general, non-rising steam gate valves are BEST adaptable for

    A. places that have plenty of head room
    B. throttling or close control
    C. places where space is a factor
    D. use where frequent adjustments are necessary

23. Of the following pressure ranges and temperature, the one for which extra heavy weight pipe and fittings are USUALLY recommended is _____ psi and 450° F.

    A. zero to 125   B. 125 to 250
    C. 250 to 375   D. 375 to 500

24. The type of valve that is generally installed in the same line with a lift check valve is a _____.

    A. gate   B. blow-off
    C. quick opening   D. globe

25. The device that is generally used to reduce high pressure steam to low pressure steam is called a

    A. pressure relief valve   B. pressure regulating valve
    C. condenser   D. by-pass control valve

26. The mains and branches of a hot water heating system should pitch up and away from the heater NOT less than _____ in 10 feet.

    A. 1"   B. 2"   C. 3"   D. 4"

27. Of the following statements regarding a *closed expansion tank,* as used in a hot water heating system, the statement which is INCORRECT is that the tank

    A. may be located above the highest radiator
    B. may be located below the lowest radiator
    C. is vented to the atmosphere
    D. is partially filled with air under pressure

28. The PRIMARY function of a feedwater heater in a steam generating plant is to

    A. supply hot water to plumbing fixtures
    B. heat and condition water fed to the boiler
    C. generate hot water for hot water radiators
    D. provide make-up steam for high pressure steam systems

29. The proper taper of standard pipe thread is MOST NEARLY _____ to the foot.

    A. 1/8"   B. 1/4"   C. 3/8"   D. 3/4"

30.

    In the above sketch, the length of the pipe (X) required is

    A. 14 3/8"   B. 15 3/8"   C. 16 5/8"   D. 17 5/8"

31. When standard weight pipe is ordered from a manufacturer, 5% of the total number of lengths ordered may be jointers. The word *jointers* in this case means MOST NEARLY

    A. pieces of pipe longer than the standard length
    B. pieces of pipe coupled together
    C. 5% *of* the lengths are extra heavy
    D. 5% of the lengths have plain ends

32. Assume a steam pressure gauge is located 10 feet above the point where it is connected to a steam header and it reads 130 psi. The actual pressure in the header is MOST NEARLY (assume one foot of water equals .433 psi) _____ psi.

    A. 120   B. 125   C. 134   D. 140

33. An escutcheon when installed by a steam fitter's helper is USUALLY a

    A. pipe support   B. metal collar
    C. reducing fitting   D. flange packing

34. In high pressure steam installations, the type of expansion joint that is USUALLY used is the 34._____

    A. non-collapsible joints
    B. U bends
    C. corrugated-metal type joints
    D. sleeve-type couplings

35. The operating principle of a Parmalee wrench is similar to a(n) 35._____

    A. stillson wrench   B. open end wrench
    C. chain tong   D. box wrench

36. Assume that a steam fitter's helper receives a salary of $114.24 a day for 250 working days. If taxes, social security, hospitalization, and pension, deducted from his salary, amounts to 16 percent of his gross pay, then his net yearly salary will be MOST NEARLY 36._____

    A. $21,192   B. $23,988   C. $27,988   D. $28,560

37. 37._____

The one of the above sketches that indicates the proper use of a wrench to turn a pipe is sketch number

    A. 1   B. 2   C. 3   D. 4

38. The MAIN purpose of using a gate valve in low pressure steam lines is USUALLY to 38._____

    A. regulate the steam pressure in the line
    B. reverse the direction of steam flow
    C. permit flow in one direction only
    D. allow full free flow

39. A flange fitting that makes a three-way pipe connection, each of which is at right angles to each other, is known as a

   A. Y branch
   B. 90° elbow
   C. taper reducer
   D. side outlet elbow

40. The proper size of stillson wrench to use when making up 1 1/2" or 2" diameter wrought iron pipe is

   A. 8"   B. 10"   C. 18"   D. 24"

41. The pitch of the steam mains of a two-pipe vapor system should NOT be less than _____ per foot.

   A. .025"   B. .05"   C. .075"   D. .10"

42. The one of the following which determines the proper thickness of flange to use when making up steam lines is

   A. expansion in the line
   B. length of pipe
   C. diameter of pipe and pressure in the line
   D. temperature of the steam

43. Assume that four (4) pieces of pipe measuring 2'1 1/4", 4'2 3/4", 5'1 9/16", and 6'3 5/8", respectively, are cut with a saw from a pipe 20'0" long. Allowing 1/16" waste for each cut, the length of the remaining pipe is MOST NEARLY

   A. 2'1 9/16"   B. 2'2 9/16"   C. 2'4 13/16"   D. 2'8 9/16"

44. One square foot of cast iron steam radiator, exposed in a normal manner and having steam at 215° F, USUALLY has an emission of _____ B.T.U. per hour.

   A. 100   B. 140   C. 200   D. 240

45. The term *hickey* refers MOST NEARLY to a

   A. device for bending pipe
   B. special type of lift fitting
   C. special fitting to hang pipe
   D. saddle that supports steam line in trench

46. When installing a globe valve in a steam line, the valve must always be installed so that the steam pressure will be against the bottom of the seat. The PRIMARY reason for this is

   A. to permit closing the valve tightly
   B. to make it easier to open with the added pressure
   C. to permit replacing the stem packing without *killing* the line
   D. because the valve seat can withstand the pressure better than the valve body

47. If one cubic inch of steel weighs 0.28 pounds, the weight, in pounds, of a steel bar 1/2" x 6" x 2'0" long is

   A. 11   B. 16   C. 20   D. 24

48. The connection known as a *Hartford loop* is USUALLY found on 48.____

    A. radiators
    B. hot water heaters
    C. unit heaters
    D. L.P. steam boilers

49. Of the following controls, the one which is known as an *actuating control* is a 49.____

    A. relay
    B. thermostat
    C. hygrostat
    D. pressure regulator

50. The purpose of a *receiver* in a compressed air system is to 50.____

    A. supply air to the air compressor
    B. filter the flow of air going to the service line
    C. store the compressed air
    D. maintain a constant pressure

KEY (CORRECT ANSWERS)

1. A	11. A	21. A	31. B	41. A
2. D	12. A	22. C	32. C	42. C
3. B	13. B	23. B	33. B	43. B
4. D	14. D	24. D	34. B	44. D
5. D	15. D	25. B	35. C	45. A
6. C	16. A	26. A	36. B	46. C
7. A	17. C	27. C	37. C	47. C
8. C	18. D	28. B	38. D	48. D
9. D	19. D	29. D	39. D	49. A
10. B	20. D	30. C	40. D	50. C

TEST 2

DIRECTIONS: Each question or incomplete statement is followed by several suggested answers or completions. Select the one that BEST answers the question or completes the statement. *PRINT THE LETTER OF THE COREECT ANSWER IN THE SPACE AT THE RIGHT.*

1. The pitch of a hacksaw blade recommended for general work in a pipe shop is USUALLY _____ teeth per inch.   1._____

   A. 14 B. 18 C. 24 D. 32

2. Assume that when fitting a screwed flange to a pipe, it is noted that the flange threads do not fit properly. The proper procedure to follow in this case is to   2._____

   A. cut new threads on the pipe
   B. tap under-size threads in the flange
   C. tap oversize threads in the flange
   D. use sufficient lamp wick at the joint to prevent leaking

3. Assume that a water column is connected to an industrial high pressure boiler with brass, extra heavy iron, or steel pipe. The MINIMUM diameter of the pipe used for these connections should be   3._____

   A. 3/8" B. 1/2" C. 5/8" D. 1"

4. In the installation of a water column to a high pressure steam boiler, crosses are generally recommended in place of ells so that   4._____

   A. a temperature gage may be installed
   B. a stand-by refill line can be hooked up
   C. the line may be easily cleaned
   D. the boiler can be easily vented

Questions 5-6.

DIRECTIONS: Questions 5 and 6 are to be answered in accordance with the sketch below showing a pipe coil installed in a two pipe high pressure steam system.

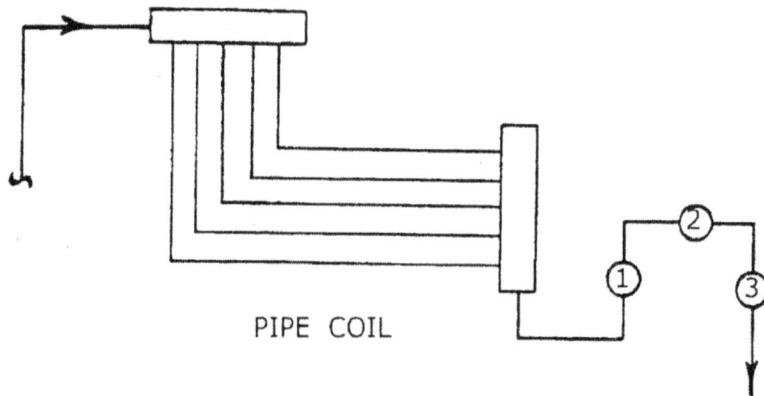

PIPE COIL

8

5. The device which is USUALLY installed at point 1 is known as a   5.____

   A. gate valve   B. float trap
   C. strainer   D. check valve

6. The device which is USUALLY installed at point 2 is known as a   6.____

   A. gate valve   B. float trap
   C. strainer   D. check valve

7. When installing a water column to a high pressure steam boiler, the bottom of the gauge   7.____
   glass should be set at _____ above the top row of tubes.

   A. 4"   B. 2"   C. 1 1/2"   D. 1"

8. A boiler feedwater regulator automatically controls the   8.____

   A. water supply to boiler
   B. water pressure to the boiler
   C. water temperature in boiler
   D. feedwater treatment to boiler

9. The MINIMUM number of gate valves needed in order to properly install a by-pass   9.____
   around a steam trap is MOST NEARLY

   A. 1   B. 2   C. 3   D. 4

10. Of the following types of tap, the one which is used to start an internal thread in a blind   10.____
    hole is a

    A. taper tap   B. bottoming tap
    C. plug tap   D. tap drill

11. Of the following types of chisels, the one that is recommended for chipping rough spots   11.____
    off flat surfaces is the _____ chisel.

    A. round nose   B. diamond nose
    C. cold   D. cape

Questions 12-16.

DIRECTIONS: Questions 12 through 16, inclusive, are to be answered by referring to the
             drawing symbols of screwed fittings and valves shown below.

12. Of the above sketches, the one representing an expansion joint is numbered 12.____
    A. 1   B. 2   C. 4   D. 5

13. Of the above sketches, the one representing an anchor is numbered 13.____
    A. 8   B. 5   C. 2   D. 1

14. Of the above sketches, the one representing a strainer is numbered 14.____
    A. 3   B. 4   C. 5   D. 9

15. Of the above sketches, the one representing a turned down elbow is numbered 15.____
    A. 5   B. 10   C. 11   D. 12

16. Of the above sketches, the one representing a thermostatic trap is 16.____
    A. 3   B. 5   C. 6   D. 9

17. Of the following devices, the one which is known as an actuating device is a 17.____
    A. damper   B. relay
    C. pressure regulator   D. control valve

18. Of the following accessories used in an air compressor system, the one that condenses water and oil vapor into a liquid is generally known as a(n) 18.____
    A. filter   B. strainer
    C. air cooled condenser   D. after cooler

19. A gauge that can be used to measure either a vacuum or pressure (p.s.i.g.) is generally called a _____ gauge. 19.____
    A. compound   B. pressure   C. boiler   D. steam

Questions 20-21.

DIRECTIONS: Questions 20 and 21 refer to the following sketch.

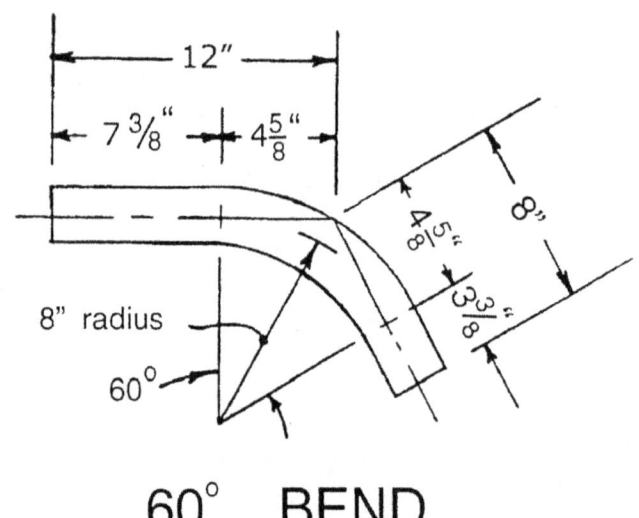

60° BEND

20. In the above sketch, if the length of the curved portion of the bend is 8 1/4" long, then the overall length of pipe needed to fabricate this bend is MOST NEARLY 20.____

    A. 18 1/2"   B. 19"   C. 20"   D. 20 1/4"

21. In the above sketch, the set-back distance is 21.____

    A. 3 3/8"   B. 4 5/8"   C. 7 3/8"   D. 12"

22. The function of a steam separator is to PRIMARILY 22.____

    A. separate the steam into two equal lines
    B. remove condensation from steam lines
    C. throttle the steam flow in the line
    D. remove oil vapor from the steam

23. Of the following steam heating systems, the one that operates under both vacuum and low pressure conditions, without using a vacuum pump, is generally known as a _____ system. 23.____

    A. one pipe low pressure   B. vacuum
    C. vapor   D. high pressure

24. Of the following metals, the one which is non-ferrous is 24.____

    A. cast iron   B. chrome-nickel
    C. copper   D. steel

25. Of the following, the one which is used to operate pneumatic tools is 25.____

    A. steam   B. compressed air
    C. water   D. oil

26. The pressure relief valve in a hot water heating system is USUALLY connected to the 26.____

    A. top of boiler   B. main header
    C. expansion tank   D. highest radiator

Questions 27-28.

DIRECTIONS: Questions 27 and 28 are based on the following paragraph.

Because of the large capacity of unit heaters, care should be taken to see that the steam piping leading to them is of sufficient size. Unit heaters should not be used on one-pipe systems. If the heating system contains direct radiators operated with steam under vacuum, it is best to have the unit heaters served by a separate main so that steam above atmospheric pressure can be supplied to the units, if desired, without interfering with the operation of the direct radiators.

27. According to the above paragraph, unit heaters are supplied with 27.____

    A. steam under vacuum
    B. steam from direct radiators
    C. separate steam lines
    D. steam preferably from a one-pipe system

28. According to the above paragraph, it may be said that unit heaters work BEST with   28._____

    A. steam above atmospheric pressure
    B. direct radiators
    C. one-pipe systems
    D. vacuum systems

Questions 29-30.

DIRECTIONS: Questions 29 and 30 are based on the following paragraph.

   Most heating units emit heat by radiation and convection. An exposed radiator emits approximately half of its heat by radiation, the amount depending upon the size and number of sections. In general, a thin radiator, such as a wall radiator, emits a larger proportion of its heat by radiation than does a thick radiator. When a radiator is enclosed or shielded, the proportion of heat emitted by radiation is reduced. The balance of the emission occurs by conduction to the air in contact with the heating surface, and this heated air rises by circulation due to convection, and transmits this warm air to the space which is to be heated.

29. According to the above paragraph, when a radiator is enclosed, a GREATER portion of   29._____
    the heat is emitted to the room by

    A. convection   B. radiation
    C. conduction   D. transmission

30. According to the above paragraph, the amount of heat that a radiator emits is   30._____

    A. approximately half of its heat by radiation
    B. determined by the thickness of the radiator
    C. dependent upon whether it is exposed or enclosed
    D. dependent upon the size and number of sections of the radiator

KEY (CORRECT ANSWERS)

1.	B	16.	B
2.	A	17.	C
3.	D	18.	D
4.	C	19.	A
5.	B	20.	B
6.	D	21.	B
7.	A	22.	B
8.	A	23.	C
9.	C	24.	C
10.	A	25.	B
11.	C	26.	A
12.	B	27.	C
13.	D	28.	A
14.	A	29.	A
15.	C	30.	D

EXAMINATION SECTION
TEST 1

DIRECTIONS: Each question or incomplete statement is followed by several suggested answers or completions. Select the one that BEST answers the question or completes the statement. *PRINT THE LETTER OF THE CORRECT ANSWER IN THE SPACE AT THE RIGHT.*

1. Steam flows through pipes because of

    A. pipe friction
    B. superheat
    C. pressure differences
    D. heat circulation

    1.____

2. The one of the following types of heating systems that should have an expansion tank is the _____ heating system.

    A. one-ipe steam
    B. hot-water
    C. mechanical warm air
    D. two-pipe steam

    2.____

3. A Hartford Loop should be connected to a

    A. standpipe
    B. forced warm-air system
    C. pipe expansion system
    D. steam boiler

    3.____

4. Whenever steam at a temperature of 230° F is to be conveyed by piping, allowances must be made for

    A. flaring
    B. corrosion
    C. expansion
    D. hardness

    4.____

5. A float and thermostatic trap would MOST likely be installed in a _____ line.

    A. fuel oil
    B. steam heating
    C. hot water
    D. compressed air

    5.____

6. A pipe fitting used for connecting four pipes that are at right angles to each other is called a

    A. branch
    B. double offset
    C. dutchman
    D. cross

    6.____

7. An intercooler is MOST often used with a(n)

    A. unit heater
    B. gear type pump
    C. oil pump
    D. air compressor

    7.____

8. A boiler bottom blow-off should be connected to the

    A. water column
    B. lowest water space available
    C. superheater
    D. steam injector

    8.____

9. A boiler feedwater regulator automatically controls the

    A. hot water temperature in the boiler
    B. water supply to the boiler

    9.____

C. water pressure to the boiler
D. feedwater treatment tank level

10. Steam at the temperature of evaporation is said to be

    A. saturated
    B. superheated
    C. dried
    D. exhausted

11. A unit heater supplies heat by

    A. gravity flow
    B. conduction
    C. forced convection
    D. negative pressure

12. The one of the following that is an accessory to a suspended gas unit heater is the

    A. vent
    B. pressure type burner
    C. drum
    D. fusible plug

13. A gasket material that can properly be used in oil applications is

    A. plain monel
    B. corrugated copper
    C. fiber
    D. asbestos composition

14. The one of the following that has the function of discharging the condensate from steam piping without permitting the steam to escape is a

    A. steam trap
    B. condenser
    C. lift valve
    D. poppet valve

15. The abbreviation CI stamped on the body of a valve represents a

    A. temperature limit
    B. seat size
    C. material designation
    D. service description

16. The one of the following types of valves usually used to throttle flow is the _____ valve.

    A. gate   B. globe   C. plug   D. ball

17. The one of the following valves that should be used to maintain a constant lower pressure in a piping system delivering steam from a higher pressure source is the _____ valve.

    A. by-pass
    B. needle
    C. impulse
    D. pressure-reducing

18. A valve that will permit water to flow in one direction only is the _____ valve.

    A. blowoff   B. angle   C. check   D. dead-end

19. The fitting that should be used to close off an opening in a pipe tee is the

    A. plug   B. cowl   C. eccentric   D. lateral

20. *Type K* is a term used in connection with a

    A. lead pipe
    B. copper tube
    C. pipe coil
    D. seamless steel tank

KEY (CORRECT ANSWERS)

1. C
2. B
3. D
4. C
5. B

6. D
7. D
8. B
9. B
10. A

11. C
12. A
13. C
14. A
15. C

16. B
17. D
18. C
19. A
20. B

TEST 2

DIRECTIONS: Each question or incomplete statement is followed by several suggested answers or completions. Select the one that BEST answers the question or completes the statement. *PRINT THE LETTER OF THE CORRECT ANSWER IN THE SPACE AT THE RIGHT.*

1. In a one-pipe steam heating system, a runout to a radiator should be taken off the steam main at an angle above the horizontal of MOST NEARLY   1.____

   A. 7°　　　B. 18°　　　C. 30°　　　D. 45°

2. The MINIMUM permitted size (diameter) of water column drain pipe for an industrial high pressure boiler is   2.____

   A. 3/4"　　　B. 9/16"　　　C. 1/2"　　　D. 1/4"

3. The pitch of a steam main for a two-pipe high pressure system should *normally* be equal to or greater than _____ inch in ten feet.   3.____

   A. 1/4　　　B. 1/8　　　C. 1/16　　　D. 1/10

4. Water hammer MOST often occurs when   4.____

   A. the size of a pipe does not increase uniformly
   B. a valve is shut suddenly
   C. there is a loss of water pressure in a pipe
   D. ice forms in a pipe due to cold weather

5. One square foot of equivalent direct radiation (E.D.R.) is defined as that amount of steam-heating surface which will deliver _____ BTU per hour.   5.____

   A. 125　　　B. 160　　　C. 240　　　D. 295

6. When a steam radiator in a one-pipe gravity system is air bound, the cause is MOST likely to be   6.____

   A. an open steam valve　　　B. a defective wedge gate
   C. a defective air valve　　　D. insufficient steam quality

7. Of the following, the one that is MOST often the cause of *knocking* in a steam pipe is   7.____

   A. rapid expansion of the steam pipe
   B. the steam is superheated
   C. a high steam temperature
   D. reverse flow of the steam in the steam line

8. When the outside of a bare pipe is coated with moisture, the pipe is *usually* carrying   8.____

   A. hot water　　　B. steam
   C. cold water　　　D. hot gas

9. *Pipe schedule number 80* refers to a pipe that is classified as   9.____

   A. double extra strong　　　B. type M
   C. extra strong　　　D. standard

18

10. The one of the following that is *generally* used to anchor a pipe support bracket to a concrete wall is the

    A. shackle
    B. blivet
    C. expansion shield
    D. mullion

11. A recess in the wall of a building, for the purpose of holding pipes which go from floor to floor, is called a

    A. closet   B. bidet   C. chase   D. cowl

12. The one of the following that can be used as an escutcheon is the

    A. flange   B. union   C. cap   D. leader

13. The one of the following types of valves that should be used when very accurate throttling is required is the _____ valve.

    A. relief   B. poppet   C. lift   D. needle

14. The letters O. S. and Y. are abbreviations for

    A. outside size wye
    B. operating shock service
    C. outside screw and yoke
    D. operating steam yoke

15. The symbols *150 SP* on a valve represent the valve's

    A. air capacity
    B. rating
    C. water capacity
    D. maintenance

16. The one of the following devices that is sensitive to changes in air temperature in a room is the

    A. rheostat
    B. thermostat
    C. damperstat
    D. aquastat

17. The *nominal* size of a 3-inch pipe refers to the pipe's

    A. inside diameter
    B. wall thickness
    C. weight per foot
    D. root diameter

18. Brass is basically made of copper and

    A. tungsten   B. antimony   C. lead   D. zinc

19. A metal formed by the combination of two or more metals is known as an

    A. anneal   B. extrusion   C. element   D. alloy

20. The MAIN element in a ferrous metal is

    A. iron   B. cadmium   C. copper   D. bismuth

KEY (CORRECT ANSWERS)

1. D
2. A
3. A
4. B
5. C

6. C
7. A
8. C
9. C
10. C

11. C
12. A
13. D
14. C
15. B

16. B
17. A
18. D
19. D
20. A

EXAMINATION SECTION
TEST 1

DIRECTIONS: Each question or incomplete statement is followed by several suggested answers or completions. Select the one that BEST answers the question or completes the statement. *PRINT THE LETTER OF THE CORRECT ANSWER IN THE SPACE AT THE RIGHT.*

Questions 1-5.

DIRECTIONS: Questions 1 through 5, inclusive, are to be answered by referring to the following symbols that would be used on a piping drawing for pipe fittings and valves.

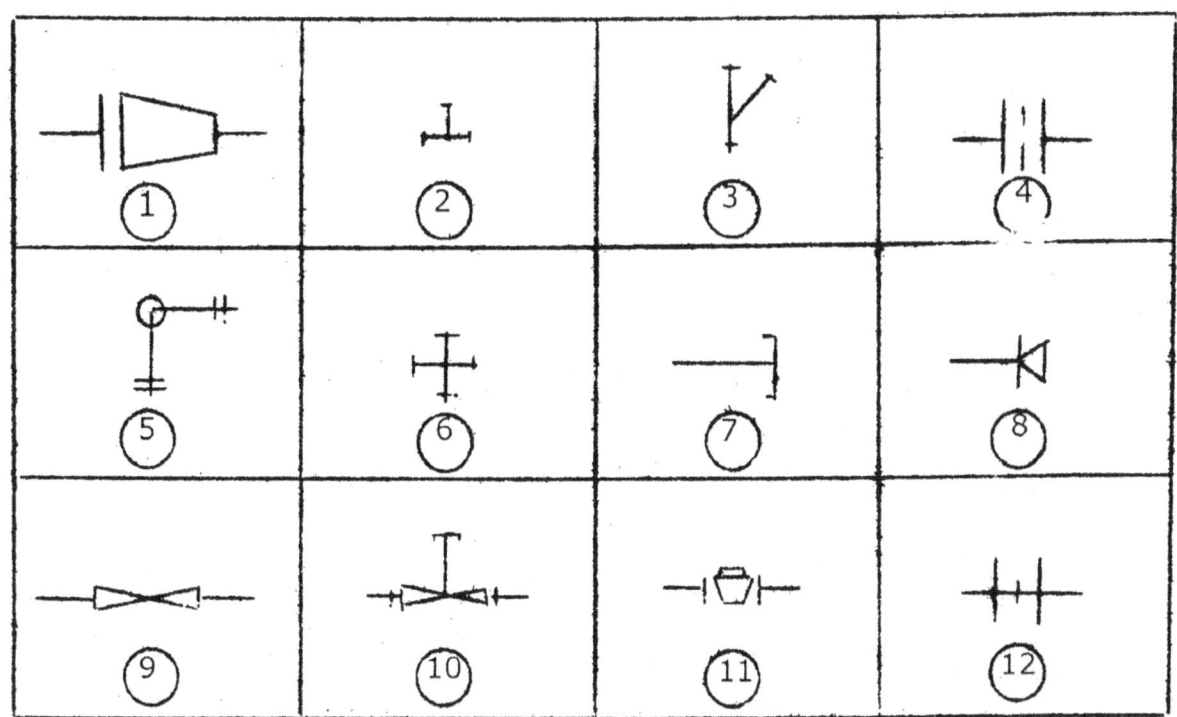

1. The symbol representing a pipe plug is numbered 1.____
   A. 1 B. 8 C. 9 D. 11

2. The symbol representing a screwed gate valve is numbered 2.____
   A. 5 B. 7 C. 9 D. 12

3. The symbol representing a union is numbered 3.____
   A. 3 B. 4 C. 8 D. 12

4. The symbol representing a reducing flange is numbered 4.____
   A. 1 B. 2 C. 5 D. 9

5. The symbol representing a screwed lateral is numbered 5.____
   A. 1 B. 3 C. 5 D. 7

6. A piping sketch is drawn to a scale of 1/8" = 1 foot. A vertical steam line measuring 3 1/2" on the sketch would have an ACTUAL length of _____ feet.

   A. 16 B. 22 C. 24 D. 28

7. Three lengths of pipe 1'10", 3'2 1/2", and 5'7 1/2", respectively, are to be cut from a pipe 14'0" long. Allowing 1/8" for each pipe cut, the length of pipe remaining is

   A. 3'1 1/8" B. 3'2 1/2" C. 3'3 1/4" D. 3'3 5/8"

8. According to the building code, the MAXIMUM permitted surface temperature of combustible construction materials located near heating equipment is

   A. 170° F B. 195° F C. 210° F D. 220° F

9. A condensate pump discharges hot condensate to a

   A. boiler B. sewer C. well D. compressor

10. A pipe with an outside diamter of 4" has a circumference of MOST NEARLY _____ inches.

    A. 8.05 B. 9.81 C. 12.57 D. 14.92

11. A steam gauge that reads 120 psi is located 20 feet below the point at which it is connected to a steam main. The pressure in the steam main is MOST NEARLY _____ psi.

    A. 111 B. 100 C. 80 D. 67

Questions 12-16.

DIRECTIONS: Questions 12 through 16, inclusive, are to be answered in accordance with the following paragraph.

The thickness of insulation necessary for the most economical results varies with the steam temperature. The standard covering consists of 85 percent magnesia with 10 percent of long-fibre asbestos as a binder. Both magnesia and laminated asbestos - felt and other forms of mineral wool including glass wool - are also used for heat insulation. The magnesia and laminated asbestos coverings may be safely used at temperatures up to 600° F. Pipe insulation is applied in molded sections 3 feet long. The sections are attached to the pipe by means of galvanized iron wire or netting. Flanges and fittings can be insulated by direct application of magnesia cement to the metal without *reinforcement*. Insulation should always be maintained in good condition because it saves fuel. Routine maintenance of warm-pipe insulation should include prompt repair of damaged surfaces. Steam and hot water leaks concealed by insulation will be difficult to detect. Underground steam or hot-water pipes are best insulated using a concrete trench with removable cover.

12. The word *reinforcement,* as used above, means MOST NEARLY

    A. resistance B. strengthening
    C. regulation D. removal

13. According to the above paragraph, magnesia and laminated asbestos coverings may be safely used at temperatures up to

    A. 800° F B. 720° F C. 675° F D. 600° F

14. According to the above paragraph, insulation should ALWAYS be maintained in good condition because it

    A. is laminated
    B. saves fuel
    C. is attached to the pipe
    D. prevents leaks

15. According to the above paragraph, pipe insulation sections are attached to the pipe by means of

    A. binders
    B. mineral wool
    C. netting
    D. staples

16. According to the above paragraph, a leak in a hot-water pipe may be difficult to detect because, when insulation is used, the leak is

    A. underground
    B. hidden
    C. routine
    D. cemented

17. The power source of a pneumatic tool is

    A. manual
    B. water pressure
    C. compressed air
    D. electricity

18. The tool used to cut internal pipe threads is a

    A. broach B. tap C. die D. rod

19. Of the following tools, the one that should be used to cut thin-wall metal tubing is the

    A. reamer B. plier C. hacksaw D. broach

20. A wrench that can be used to tighten a nut to a specified tightness is a _____ wrench.

    A. bonney
    B. spud
    C. torque
    D. adjustable

KEY (CORRECT ANSWERS)

1.	B	11.	A
2.	C	12.	B
3.	D	13.	D
4.	A	14.	B
5.	B	15.	C
6.	D	16.	B
7.	D	17.	C
8.	A	18.	B
9.	A	19.	C
10.	C	20.	C

TEST 2

DIRECTIONS: Each question or incomplete statement is followed by several suggested answers or completions. Select the one that BEST answers the question or completes the statement. *PRINT THE LETTER OF THE CORRECT ANSWER IN THE SPACE AT THE RIGHT.*

1. The one of the following that will MOST likely show a *mushroomed* head is a 1.____

    A. cold chisel B. file cleaner
    C. screwdriver blade D. ratchet

2. A tool that is used to bend pipe is the 2.____

    A. lintel B. hickey C. collet D. brace

3. Of the following types of fire extinguishers, the one that should be used to extinguish an electrical fire is the _____ fire extinguisher. 3.____

    A. soda acid B. foam
    C. carbon dioxide D. water

4. The MAIN reason for grounding electrical equipment is to 4.____

    A. increase power to the coils
    B. increase wattage in the line
    C. prevent serious short circuits
    D. protect personnel from electrical shock

5. When disconnecting the electric wires from a motor, it is GOOD practice to 5.____

    A. cut the live power wires
    B. assume that the circuit is alive
    C. scrape the terminals
    D. nick the wire in several places first

6. A SAFE procedure to follow when using a straight-type ladder is to 6.____

    A. use a box or stair to support the ladder legs
    B. hang tools on the ladder so they cannot be dropped
    C. take one step at a time when climbing
    D. have an assistant climb behind you to protect you

7. Safety in work habits is MOST closely related to which of the following? 7.____

    A. Worker's knowledge of the job
    B. Speed with which a worker does the job
    C. Wages paid to a worker
    D. Carefulness of a worker

8. When a helper drops oil onto a plant floor, he should 8.____

    A. find out who is supposed to clean it up
    B. inform the foreman
    C. dry it up himself
    D. let it soak into the floor

9. Assume that a helper earns $5.58 an hour and that he works 250 seven-hour days a year. His gross yearly salary will be

   A. $9,715   B. $9,765   C. $9,825   D. $9,890

10. A pipe having an inside diameter of 3.48 inches and a wall thickness of .18 inches will have an outside diameter of _____ inches.

    A. 3.84   B. 3.64   C. 3.57   D. 3.51

11. A rectangular steel bar having a volume of 30 cubic inches, a width of 2 inches, and a height of 3 inches will have a length of _____ inches.

    A. 12   B. 10   C. 8   D. 5

12. A pipe weighs 20.4 pounds per foot of length. The TOTAL weight of eight pieces of this pipe with each piece 20 feet in length is MOST NEARLY _____ pounds.

    A. 460   B. 1,680   C. 2,420   D. 3,260

13. According to the building code, all portions of standpipe systems should be painted

    A. black   B. red   C. blue   D. yellow

14. According to the building code, a material acceptable for the fittings of a fire standpipe system above ground is

    A. copper
    B. chromium
    C. malleable brass
    D. cast steel

15. According to the building code, an uninsulated steam pipe must be a MINIMUM clear distance from combustible materials of _____ inch.

    A. 1/2   B. 1/4   C. 1/8   D. 1/16

Questions 16-20.

DIRECTIONS: Questions 16 through 20, inclusive, are to be answered in accordance with the following paragraph.

Reductions in pipe size of a building heating system are made with eccentric fittings and are pitched downward. The ends of mains with gravity return shall be at least 18" above the water line of the boiler. As condensate flows opposite to the steam runouts are one size larger than the vertical pipe and are pitched upward. In a one-pipe system, an automatic air vent must be provided at each main to relieve air pressure and to let steam enter the radiator. As steam enters the radiator, a *thermal* device causes the vent to close, thereby holding the steam. Steam mains should not be less than two inches in diameter. The end of the steam main should have a minimum size of one-half of its greatest diameter. Small steam systems should be sized for a 2 oz. pressure drop. Large steam systems should be sized for a 4 oz. pressure drop.

16. The word *thermal,* as used in the above paragraph, means MOST NEARLY

    A. convector   B. heat   C. instrument   D. current

17. According to the above paragraph, the one of the following that is one size larger than the vertical pipe is the

   A. steam main
   B. valve
   C. water line
   D. runout

17._____

18. According to the above paragraph, small steam systems should be sized for a pressure drop of _____ oz.

   A. 2   B. 3   C. 4   D. 5

18._____

19. According to the above paragraph, ends of mains with gravity return shall be AT LEAST

   A. 18" above the water line of the boiler
   B. one-quarter of the greatest diameter of the main
   C. twice the size of the vertical pipe in the main
   D. 18" above the steam line of the boiler

19._____

20. According to the above paragraph, the one of the following that is provided at each main to relieve air pressure is a(n)

   A. gravity return
   B. convector
   C. eccentric
   D. vent

20._____

KEY (CORRECT ANSWERS)

1. A
2. B
3. C
4. D
5. B

6. C
7. D
8. C
9. B
10. A

11. D
12. D
13. B
14. D
15. A

16. B
17. D
18. A
19. A
20. D

EXAMINATION SECTION
TEST 1

DIRECTIONS: Each question consists of a statement. You are to indicate whether the statement is TRUE (T) or FALSE (F). *PRINT THE LETTER OF THE CORRECT ANSWER IN THE SPACE AT THE RIGHT.*

1. The number of bolts used in a standard class 125, 3" pipe diameter companion flange is 4.   1._____

2. A pump is said to develop a pressure head of 8 feet of water. This is equivalent to a pressure of 18.4 lbs. per sq. in.   2._____

3. One of the principal uses of the *degree-day* is in predicting fuel consumption for a particular building for a particular period.   3._____

4. The capacity or size of many L.P. heating boilers is rated on a net (I.B.R.) rating. The abbreviation I.B.R. stands for *industrial boiler rating*.   4._____

5. A particular vacuum pump maintains a vacuum of 5 1/2 inches of mercury in the condensate return line. This is equivalent to a *negative* pressure of 2.37 lbs. per sq. in.   5._____

6. It is considered GOOD practice to run the condensate from a high pressure drip trap directly to the vacuum return line leading to the vacuum pump.   6._____

7. In the average vacuum heating system, the vacuum pump is controlled by a vacuum regulator and a float control.   7._____

8. It is generally considered POOR practice to exceed a 2-ounce pressure drop per 100 feet of equivalent run of an L.P. steam main in a vacuum return steam heating system.   8._____

9. The operating principle of the *upright bucket* trap and the *inverted bucket* trap is the same.   9._____

10. The proper installation of an inverted bucket trap, in clearing H.P. steam lines and heating appliances of condensate, should include installation of AT LEAST 2 gate valves and a strainer.   10._____

11. It is good practice to pitch L.P. steam heating mains *not less than* 1 inch in 40 feet.   11._____

12. If a steam main, 120 ft. long, is run with a pitch of 3/8" in 10 feet and the high point of the main is at an elevation of +1.250' in order to clear the soffit of the floor beams, the elevation of the top of the other end of the main will be *approximately* +0.875'.   12._____

13. The proper type of trap to use in draining the condensate from high pressure blast coils and heaters is a float and hydrostatic trap.   13._____

14. A closed float trap is the *appropriate* type of trap to use to drain low pressure steam mains at points where the main rises or where condensate only is to be handled.   14._____

15. In selecting the proper size of pressure reducing valve to use, it is BEST to choose a larger-size valve than a smaller one, where the final pressure is less than 58% of initial pressure.   15._____

16. Schedule 40 steel pipe has the same physical dimensions as double extra heavy pipe. 16._____

17. An oxy-acetylene torch is often used in cutting out existing steel pipe when making repairs. In using this equipment, one should *always* set the oxygen pressure higher than the acetylene pressure. 17._____

18. When selecting a tip for an oxy-acetylene cutting torch, a *good* rule of thumb is to select a higher numbered tip for burning lighter gauge metal. 18._____

19. If a fitter wants to drill and tap a casting to tie in a 3/4" line, he should FIRST use a 3/4" drill or hole cutter in order to get a full thread. 19._____

20. In general, heating distribution systems which take their supply from the exhausts of non-condensing steam engines are *high pressure* systems. 20._____

21. Oil heaters (steam) and oil starting heaters (electric) are *usually* installed with fixed relief valves. 21._____

Questions 22-25.

DIRECTIONS: Questions 22 through 25, inclusive, are to be answered in accordance with the following paragraph.

In district heating work for the distribution of steam, the pressure at which the steam is to be distributed will depend upon (1) boiler pressure, (2) whether exhaust or live steam, (3) pressure requirements of apparatus to be served. If steam has been passed through electrical generating units, the pressure will be considerably lower than if live steam, direct from the boiler, is used. The advantages of low pressure distribution (2 to 30 psi) are (1) smaller heat loss per square foot of pipe surface, (2) less trouble with traps and valves, (3) simpler problems in pressure reduction at the building, and (4) general reduction in maintenance costs. The advantages of high pressure distribution are (1) smaller pipe sizes, (2) greater adaptability, (3) wider flexibility.

22. With reference to the above paragraph, the heat loss per square foot of pipe surface is *inversely proportional* to the steam pressure. 22._____

23. With reference to the above paragraph, high pressure systems have a *lower* maintenance cost than low pressure systems. 23._____

24. The distribution system which should have a *lower* trap maintenance charge is the high pressure system. 24._____

25. The distribution system which must use comparatively *larger* pipe sizes is the lower pressure system. 25._____

KEY (CORRECT ANSWERS)

1. T
2. F
3. T
4. F
5. F

6. F
7. T
8. T
9. F
10. T

11. T
12. T
13. F
14. T
15. F

16. F
17. T
18. F
19. F
20. F

21. T
22. F
23. F
24. F
25. T

TEST 2

DIRECTIONS: Each question consists of a statement. You are to indicate whether the statement is TRUE (T) or FALSE (F). *PRINT THE LETTER OF THE CORRECT ANSWER IN THE SPACE AT THE RIGHT.*

1. A mechanical pressure atomizing type fuel oil burner uses No. 6 fuel oil. The fuel oil pump for this burner should deliver oil at a pressure of 75 lbs. per sq. in. 1.____

2. In an entire fuel oil piping system for units designed to burn No. 6 oil, only a *single* set of duplex straiters need be furnished and piped between the oil pump and oil heaters, in keeping with good practice. 2.____

3. In the city, steam heating plants operating in excess of 10 lbs. per sq. in. are considered high pressure plants for purposes of boiler inspection. 3.____

4. An apprentice receiving a salary of $36 for 5 1/3 hours on the job receives $6 3/4 per hour. 4.____

5. Considering that cutting consumes 1 1/2" of material, the length of 3/4" brass pipe required to make 12 nipples each 4 1/2" long is 60". 5.____

6. If the condensate in a return pipe flows at an average rate of 13 gal/hr. for 9 hours per day, then 351 gallons will flow in 3 days. 6.____

7. Four steamfitters worked on one job. In order to complete this job, each put in the following number of hours: 1st man - 6 1/2 hours, 2nd man - 5 3/4 hours, 3rd man - 7 1/4 hours, 4th man - 6 3/4 hours.
The total number of hours put in by the men is 25 1/4. 7.____

8. Assume that the formula to find the amount of water a pump will deliver is: 8.____
    $G = D^2 \times C \times S \times N \times T$, where
    G - Gallons pumped per hour
    D - Diameter of pump cylinder in inches
    C - .0408 (contents of 1" cylinder 1 foot long)
    S - Length of stroke in feet
    N - Number of strokes per minute
    T - Time expressed in minutes
If a 3" diameter pump with a 7" stroke works at the rate of 30 strokes per minute, then, in one hour, this pump will deliver 4626.72 gallons.

9. When exhaust steam from an industrial process is used for heating purposes, an extractor or separator should be used in order to catch and release air and water. 9.____

10. The capacity rating of a steam trap selected should *always* be somewhat more than the actual amount of conden-sate to be handled. 10.____

11. For efficient operation, each piece of equipment using steam should be trapped *individually* to insure positive circulation and proper air elimination. 11.____

12. The height that a steam trap is capable of elevating condensate is dependent *only* on the amount of back pressure in the return. 12.____

13. It is *important* that entrained air in the coils of unit heaters be quickly removed not only for quick heating and maximum efficiency but to get air out of the coil to prevent trouble due to corrosion.   13.____

14. Piping won't stand up and work efficiently without adequate support on strapping. Ample pipe hangers or supports on approximately 15-foot centers is considered *good* rule-of-thumb practice for the ordinary installation.   14.____

Questions 15-20.

DIRECTIONS: The figure on the next page shows some of piping and equipment mounted on or tied into a heating boiler. Questions 15 through 20, inclusive, relate to the piping and equipment shown in this sketch.

15. The letter A indicates breeching on which safety valves are *commonly* mounted.   15.____

16. The letter B shows location at which bottom blowdown is *usually* tied in.   16.____

17. The letter C indicates a symbol which represents a horizontal swing check valve.   17.____

18. The letter D shows the location at which make-up water is fed into the boiler.   18.____

19. The letter E shows the operating boiler water level.   19.____

20. The letter F points to a heat exchanger which is piped to take live steam from this boiler.   20.____

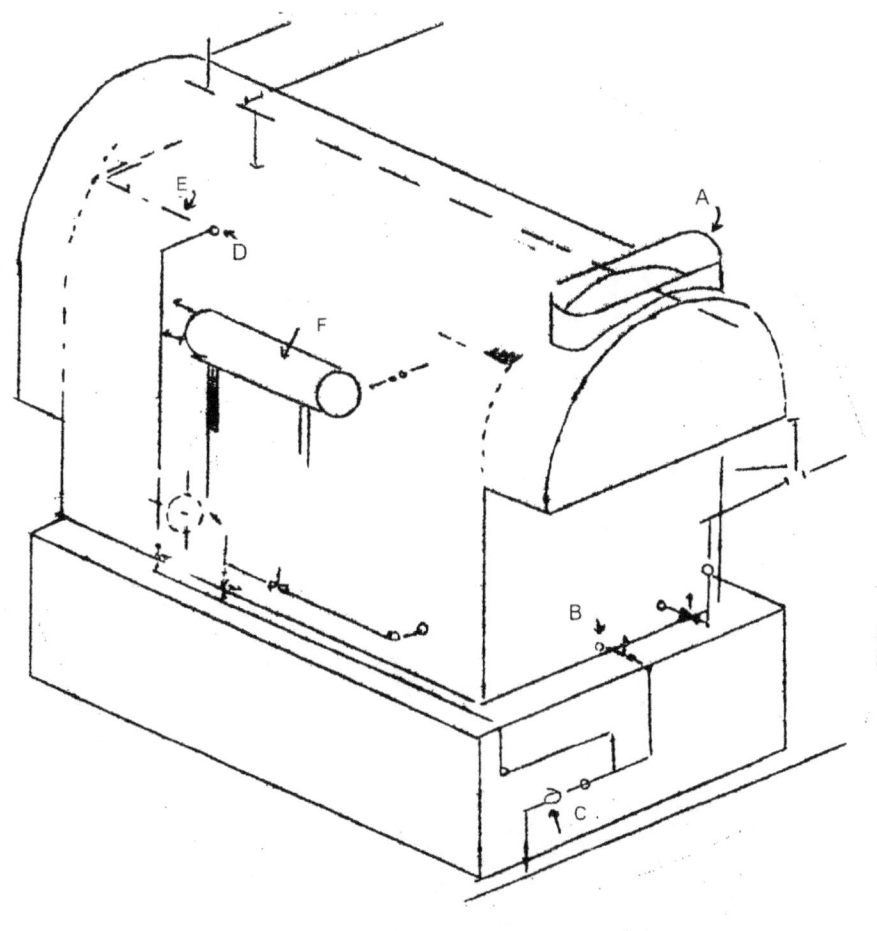

KEY (CORRECT ANSWERS)

1. F
2. F
3. F
4. T
5. F

6. T
7. F
8. F
9. F
10. T

11. T
12. F
13. T
14. F
15. F

16. T
17. F
18. F
19. T
20. F

EXAMINATION SECTION
TEST 1

DIRECTIONS: Each question or incomplete statement is followed by several suggested answers or completions. Select the one that BEST answers the question or completes the statement. *PRINT THE LETTER OF THE CORRECT ANSWER IN THE SPACE AT THE RIGHT.*

1. The combustion efficiency of a boiler can be determined with a CO_2 indicator and the   1.____

    A. under fire draft
    B. boiler room humidity
    C. flue gas temperature
    D. outside air temperature

2. A quick, practical method of determining if the cast-iron waste pipe delivered to a job has been damaged in transit is to   2.____

    A. hydraulically test it
    B. "ring" each length with a hammer
    C. drop each length to see whether it breaks
    D. visually examine the pipe for cracks

3. An electrostatic precipitator is used to   3.____

    A. filter the air supply
    B. remove sludge from the fuel oil
    C. remove particles from the fuel gas
    D. supply samples for an Orsat analysis

4. The PRIMARY cause of cracking and spalling of refractory lining in the furnace of a steam generator is *most likely* due to   4.____

    A. continuous over-firing of boiler
    B. slag accumulation on furnace walls
    C. change in fuel from solid to liquid
    D. uneven heating and cooling within the refractory brick

5. The term "effective temperature" in air conditioning means   5.____

    A. the dry bulb temperature
    B. the average of the wet and dry bulb temperatures
    C. the square root of the product of wet and dry bulb temperatures
    D. an arbitrary index combining the effects of temperature, humidity, and movement

6. The piping in all buildings having dual water distribution systems should be identified by a color coding of _____ for potable water lines and _____ for non-potable water lines.   6.____

    A. green; red
    B. green; yellow
    C. yellow; green
    D. yellow; red

7. The breaking of a component of a machine subjected to excessive vibration is called   7.____

    A. tensile failure
    B. fatigue failure
    C. caustic embrittlement
    D. amplitude failure

8. The TWO MOST important factors to be considered in selecting fans for ventilating systems are

   A. noise and efficiency
   B. space available and weight
   C. first cost and dimensional bulk
   D. construction and arrangement of drive

9. In the modern power plant deaerator, air is removed from water to

   A. reduce heat losses in the heaters
   B. reduce corrosion of boiler steel due to the air
   C. reduce the load of the main condenser air pumps
   D. prevent pumps from becoming vapor bound

10. The abbreviations BOD, COD, and DO are associated with

    A. flue gas analysis
    B. air pollution control
    C. boiler water treatment
    D. water pollution control

11. The piping of a newly installed drainage system should be tested upon completion of the rough plumbing with a head of water of NOT LESS THAN _____ feet.

    A. 10   B. 15   C. 20   D. 25

12. Of the following statements concerning aquastats, the one which is CORRECT is:

    A. Aquastats may be obtained with either a narrow or wide range of settings
    B. Aquastats have a mercury tube switch which is controlled by the stack switch
    C. An aquastat is a device used to shut down the burner in the event of low water in the boiler
    D. An aquastat should be located about 4 inches above the normal water line of the boiler

13. The SAFEST way to protect the domestic water supply from contamination by sewage or non-potable water is to insert

    A. air gaps
    B. swing connections
    C. double check valves
    D. tanks with overhead discharge

14. The MAIN function of a back-pressure valve which is sometimes found in the connection between a water drain pipe and the sewer system is to

    A. equalize the pressure between the drain pipe and the sewer
    B. prevent sewer water from flowing into the drain pipe
    C. provide pressure to enable waste to reach the sewer
    D. make sure that there is not too much water pressure in the sewer line

15. Boiler water is neutral if its pH value is

    A. 0   B. 1   C. 7   D. 14

16. A domestic hot water mixing or tempering valve should be preceded in the hot water line by a

   A. strainer
   B. foot valve
   C. check valve
   D. steam trap

17. Between a steam boiler and its safety valve there should be

   A. no valve of any type
   B. a gate valve of the same size as the safety valve
   C. a swing check valve of at least the same size as the safety valve
   D. a cock having a clear opening equal in area to the pipe connecting the boiler and safety valve

18. A diagram of horizontal plumbing drainage lines should have cleanouts shown

   A. at least every 25 feet
   B. at least every 100 feet
   C. wherever a basin is located
   D. wherever a change in direction occurs

19. When a Bourdon gauge is used to measure steam pressures, some form of siphon or water seal must be maintained.
    The reason for this is to

   A. obtain "absolute" pressure readings
   B. prevent steam from entering the gage
   C. prevent condensate from entering the gage
   D. obtain readings below atmospheric pressure

20. In a closed heat exchanger, oil is cooled by condensate which is to be returned to a boiler. In order to avoid the possibility of contaminating the condensate with oil should a tube fail in the oil cooler, it would be good practice to

   A. cool the oil by air instead of water
   B. treat the condensate with an oil solvent
   C. keep the oil pressure in the exchanger higher than the water pressure
   D. keep the water pressure in the exchanger higher than the oil pressure

21. A radiator thermostatic trap is used on a vacuum return type of heating system to

   A. release the pocketed air only
   B. reduce the amount of condensate
   C. maintain a predetermined radiator water level
   D. prevent the return of live steam to the return line

22. According to the color coding of piping, fire protection piping should be painted

   A. green   B. yellow   C. purple   D. red

23. The MAIN purpose of a standpipe system is to

   A. supply the roof water tank
   B. provide water for firefighting

C. circulate water for the heating system
D. provide adequate pressure for the water supply

24. The name "Saybolt" is associated with the measurement of

    A. viscosity
    B. Btu content
    C. octane rating
    D. temperature

25. Recirculation of conditioned air in an air-conditioned building is done MAINLY to

    A. reduce refrigeration tonnage required
    B. increase room entrophy
    C. increase air specific humidity
    D. reduce room temperature below the dewpoint

26. In a plumbing installation, vent pipes are GENERALLY used to

    A. prevent the loss of water seal from traps by evaporation
    B. prevent the loss of water seal due to several causes other than evaporation
    C. act as an additional path for liquids to flow through during normal use of a plumbing fixture
    D. prevent the backflow of water in a cross-connection between a drinking water line and a sewage line

27. The designation "150 W" cast on the bonnet of a gate valve is an indication of the

    A. water working temperature
    B. water working pressure
    C. area of the opening in square inches
    D. weight of the valve in pounds

28. In the city, the size soil pipe necessary in a sewage drainage system is determined by the

    A. legal occupancy of the building
    B. vertical height of the soil line
    C. number of restrooms connected to the soil line
    D. number of "fixture units" connected to the soil line

29. Fins or other extended surfaces are used on heat exchanger tubes when

    A. the exchanger is a water-to-water exchanger
    B. water is on one side of the tube and condensing steam on the other side
    C. the surface coefficient of heat transfer on both sides of the tube is high
    D. the surface coefficient of heat transfer on one side of the tube is low compared to the coefficient on the other side of the tube

30. A fusible plug may be put in a fire tube boiler as an emergency device to indicate low water level. The fusible plug is installed so that under normal operating conditions,

    A. both sides are exposed to steam
    B. one side is exposed to water and the other side to steam
    C. one side is exposed to steam and the other side to hot gases
    D. one side is exposed to the water and the other side to hot gases

5 (#1)

31. Extra strong wrought-iron pipe, as compared to standard wrought-iron pipe of the same nominal size, has

    A. the same outside diameter but a smaller inside diameter
    B. the same inside diameter but a larger outside diameter
    C. a larger outside diameter and a smaller inside diameter
    D. larger inside and outside diameters

31._____

32. Fans may be rated on a dynamic or a static efficiency basis. The dynamic efficiency would *probably* be

    A. lower in value because of the energy absorbed by the air velocity
    B. the same as the static in the case of centrifugal blowers running at various speeds
    C. the same as the static in the case of axial flow blowers running at various speeds
    D. higher in value than the static

32._____

33. The function of the stack relay in an oil burner installation is to

    A. regulate the draft over the fire
    B. regulate the flow of fuel oil to the burner
    C. stop the motor if the oil has not ignited
    D. stop the motor if the water or steam pressure is too high

33._____

34. The type of centrifugal pump which is inherently balanced for hydraulic thrust is the

    A. double suction impeller type
    B. single suction impeller type
    C. single stage type
    D. multistage type

34._____

35. The specifications for a job using sheet lead calls for "4-lb. sheet lead."
    This means that each sheet should weigh

    A. 4 lbs.   B. 4 lbs. per square
    C. 4 lbs. per square foot   D. 4 lbs. per cubic inch

35._____

36. The total cooling load design conditions for a building are divided for convenience into two components.
    These are:

    A. infiltration and radiation
    B. sensible heat and latent heat
    C. wet and dry bulb temperatures
    D. solar heat gain and moisture transfer

36._____

37. The function of a Hartford loop used on some steam boilers is to

    A. limit boiler steam pressure
    B. limit temperature of the steam
    C. prevent high water levels in the boiler
    D. prevent back flow of water from the boiler into the return main

37._____

38. Vibration from a ventilating blower can be prevented from being transmitted to the duct work by

    A. installing straighteners in the duct
    B. throttling the air supply to the blower
    C. bolting the blower tightly to the duct
    D. installing a canvas sleeve at the blower outlet

39. A specification states that access panels to suspended ceiling will be of metal. The MAIN reason for providing access panels is to

    A. improve the insulation of the ceiling
    B. improve the appearance of the ceiling
    C. make it easier to construct the building
    D. make it easier to maintain the building

40. A plumber on a job reports that the steamfitter has installed a 3" steam line in a location at which the plans show the house trap. On inspecting the job, you should

    A. tell the steamfitter to remove the steam line
    B. study the condition to see if the house trap can be relocated
    C. tell the plumber and steamfitter to work it out between themselves and then report to you
    D. tell the plumber to find another location for the trap because the steamfitter has already completed his work

41. In the installation of any heating system, the MOST important consideration is that

    A. all elements be made of a good grade of cast iron
    B. all radiators and connectors be mounted horizontally
    C. the smallest velocity of flow of heating medium be used
    D. there be proper clearance between hot surfaces and surrounding combustible material

42. Which one of the following is the PRIMARY object in drawing up a set of specifications for materials to be purchased?

    A. Control of quality
    B. Outline of intended use
    C. Establishment of standard sizes
    D. Location and method of inspection.

43. The drawing which should be used as a LEGAL reference when checking completed construction work is the _____ drawing.

    A. contract   B. assembly
    C. working or shop   D. preliminary

Questions 44-50.

DIRECTIONS: Questions 44 through 50 refer to the plumbing drawing shown below.

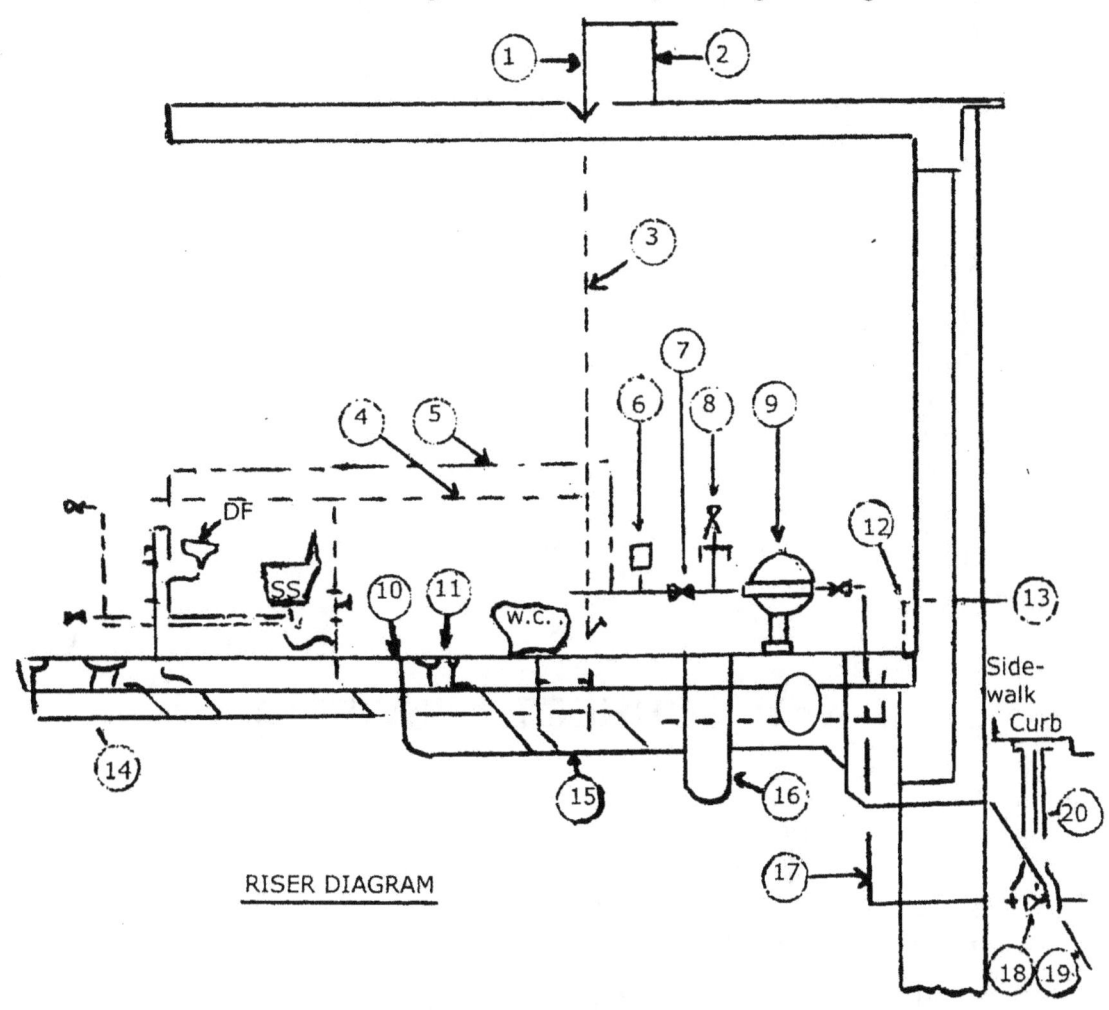

RISER DIAGRAM

44. According to the building code, the MINIMUM diameter of No. ① and its minimum height, No. ② respectively, are

    A. 2" and 12"
    B. 3" and 18"
    C. 4" and 24"
    D. 6" and 36"

44.____

45. No. ⑥ is a

    A. relief valve
    B. shock absorber
    C. testing connection
    D. drain

45.____

46. No. ⑨ is a

    A. strainer
    B. float valve
    C. meter
    D. pedestal

46.____

47. No. ⑪ is a

    A. floor drain
    B. cleanout
    C. trap
    D. vent connection

47.____

48. No. ⑬ is a

    A. standpipe
    C. sprinkler head
    B. air inlet
    D. cleanout

49. The size of No. ⑯ is

    A. 2" x 2"
    C. 3" x 3"
    B. 2" x 3"
    D. 4" x 4"

50. No. ⑱ is a

    A. pressure reducing valve
    B. butterfly valve
    C. curb cock
    D. sprinkler head

KEY (CORRECT ANSWERS)

1. C	11. A	21. D	31. A	41. D
2. B	12. C	22. D	32. D	42. A
3. C	13. A	23. B	33. C	43. A
4. D	14. B	24. A	34. A	44. C
5. D	15. C	25. A	35. C	45. B
6. B	16. A	26. B	36. B	46. C
7. B	17. A	27. B	37. D	47. A
8. A	18. D	28. D	38. D	48. B
9. B	19. B	29. D	39. D	49. D
10. D	20. D	30. D	40. B	50. C

EXAMINATION SECTION
TEST 1

DIRECTIONS: Answer the following questions directly, briefly, and succinctly.

1. What is the device called that supports a riser and holds it rigidly to a fixed point?

2. What gases are MOST commonly used in welding?

3. What kind of fitting is used to reduce the size of a main?

4. What effect does a vacuum have on the boiling point of water in a common steam heating apparatus?

5. What kind of pipe is preferable for underground work?

6. What is a radiator breaking bar used for?

7. Name three common methods of connecting pipes and fittings.

8. Why are traps put on steam lines?

9. When exhaust steam is used for heating purposes, what takes the grease and oil out of the steam?

10. What is the difference between a direct-indirect radiator and a direct radiator?

KEY (CORRECT ANSWERS)

1. Anchor (clamp)
   Hanger

2. Oxygen
   Acetylene

3. Reducer (eccentric reducer)

4. Lowers it

5. Wrought iron
   Black iron
   Copper

6. Assemble (or disassemble) radiators

7. Welded
   Flanged (riveted)
   Threaded (screwed)

8. To catch and release air (or water)

9. Extractor (separator) (grease trap)

10. Direct-indirect heats air from outside
    Direct heats air in the room

TEST 2

DIRECTIONS: Answer the following questions directly, briefly, and succinctly,

1. What is the standard push or slip nipple used for?

2. What are the two MOST common methods of welding?

3. What is the difference between dry returns and wet returns?

4. Name two ways that water of condensation is returned to the boilers in large plants where high-pressure boilers are used.

5. What kind of pipe is used on high-pressure boilers?

6. What is the usual pressure in a low-pressure heating system?

7. What two kinds of pipe are MOST commonly used for steam installation?

8. When ordering a reducing tee, what is the right way to give the size of the outlets?

9. Where is the dirt pockets installed?

10. Which gas is turned off first when putting out the flames on an acetylene torch?

KEY (CORRECT ANSWERS)

1. Radiators
   Boilers

2. Acetylene (gas)
   Electric (arc)

3. Dry above water line
   Wet below water line

4. Pumps
   Traps
   Injectors

5. Steel (extra heavy)

6. 1 to 10 pounds

7. Steel
   Wrought iron
   Black iron

8. Run first, and side (branch) (bullhead) last
   Read through the tee

9. End (lowest part) of main
   Bottom of risers

10. Acetylene

TEST 3

DIRECTIONS: Answer the following questions directly, briefly, and succinctly.

1. What kind of joints are used in pipe for high-pressure boilers?

2. What is the steam pipe called that is connected to the top of the boiler and carried horizontally on basement ceiling?

3. What is the vertical pipe called that supplies the steam to various floors?

4. In welding two pieces of metal greater than 1/4 inch in thickness, what is done to the edges?

5. How high above the boiler water line should the end of the supply main be in a one-pipe gravity-feed system with a wet return?

6. What is used to avoid air pockets in a steam line?

7. On how small a variation in temperature should a thermostat react?

8. With what is the contraction and expansion of long straight runs of pipe taken care of?

9. What fitting is used to make a short elbow connection?

10. Name two kinds of coils made from pipe.

2 (#3)

KEY (CORRECT ANSWERS)

1. Flanged
   Welded
   Threaded

2. Steam main (loop)
   Header
   Feed line

3. Riser

4. Bevel (taper)

5. Not less than 18 inches

6. Vents
   Traps

7. 2 to 5 degrees

8. Expansion (slip) joint
   Expansion bend (loop)

9. Street ell
   Service elbow

10. Mitre
    Spiral
    Corner
    Return bends
    Manifold (header)

TEST 4

DIRECTIONS: Answer the following questions directly, briefly, and succinctly.

1. How many sections are there in the rear section of a sectional boiler?

2. What ell would one use for connecting branches to steam mains?

3. What is used to hold asbestos blocks in place around a boiler?

4. What does an altitude gauge measure?

5. What is used to allow the air to escape for fast circulation in a steam system?

6. What is the part of a hot water boiler called to which the smoke pipe is attached?

7. What does one call the tee having a larger branch than the run?

8. What type of system is used in a building so located with respect to the boiler plant that lifts are necessary in the return piping?

9. What is the bottom outlets of a steam boiler called?

10. What does one place above the water columns?

2 (#4)

KEY (CORRECT ANSWERS)

1. One
   Two

2. 45-degree
   90-degree

3. Wire (wire mesh) (chicken wire)

4. Height of water

5. Quick vent (air vent) (air valve)

6. Smoke hood (dome) (collar) (outlet) (box) (bonnet) (breeching)

7. Bullhead
   Reducing tee

8. Vacuum
   Forced flow (pressure)
   Pump

9. Returns

10. Steam gauge (pressure gauge) (gauge)
    Relief valve (safety valve) (blow-off)

———

TEST 5

DIRECTIONS: Answer the following questions directly, briefly, and succinctly.

1. What return system is below the boiler water level?

2. What are the valves on a water column called?

3. What is the system called in which the distributing main is located in the attic and the return main in the basement?

4. What is used to remove oil or other impurities from feed water?

5. Name two types of hot-water systems.

6. What is the large drip pipe called that connects the header of a boiler with a return?

KEY (CORRECT ANSWERS)

1. Wet return

2. Gauge cocks (try cocks) (pet cocks)

3. Overhead (down-feed) system

4. Separator (filter) (strainer)
   Boiler compound
   Soda (sal soda)
   Vinegar

5. Gravity
   Forced flow (forced feed) (pressure)
   Circulation
   Open
   Closed

6. Equalizer
   Bleeder
   Hartford loop

EXAMINATION SECTION
TEST 1

DIRECTIONS: Answer the following questions directly, briefly, and succinctly.

1. What piece of equipment is used to return condensed steam to the boiler?
2. What term is used when speaking of the distance that a valve covers the port on a steam engine?
3. What two types of tubes are commonly used in steam boilers?
4. What is the moving part of an A.C. motor called?
5. By what unit of measurement is one charged for ammonia gas?
6. What is opened on a centrifugal pump to see if it is air-bound?
7. What is the purpose of the condenser coils in an ammonia refrigerating system?
8. What two chemical salts are used MOST commonly in making refrigerating brines?
9. What is the instrument called that is placed on a steam engine to obtain a diagram of the pressure of the cylinder?
10. Name two different types (not makes) of safety valves.

2 (#1)

KEY (CORRECT ANSWERS)

1. Pump

2. Lap

3. Water
   Fire

4. Rotor
   Armature

5. Pound

6. Air (pet) (try) (cock)

7. Liquify (cool) (condense) ammonia or gas

8. Sodium chloride (salt)
   Calcium chloride

9. Indicator

10. Pop (spring)
    Weight (lever)

———

TEST 2

DIRECTIONS: Answer the following questions directly, briefly, and succinctly.

1. In what units are measurements of vacuum pressure given?
2. What is the part of the rotor on a D.C. motor called on which the brushes ride?
3. What kind of current can one assume was being generated if the knowledge that a generator had a commutator?
4. What is the boiling over of the water in a boiler called?
5. In what kind of refrigeration does one use higher pressures than with ammonia?
6. What is the part of the boiler called that receives the impurities of the water?
7. What instrument is used to test the quality of the flue gas?
8. What safety device besides a regulation safety valve is required on a steam boiler?
9. What will happen if dirty water is used in the boiler?
10. What type of engine is driven by jets of high-pressure steam forced against blades on a flywheel?

KEY (CORRECT ANSWERS)

1. Inches (inches of mercury)
2. Commutator
3. Direct current (D.C.)
4. Priming (foaming)
5. Carbon dioxide (CO_2) Freon
6. Mud drum (ring) (pan)
7. Orsat
   CO_2 (carbon dioxide) indicator
8. Fusible (soft) (safety) plug
9. Prime (foam)
10. Turbine

———

TEST 3

DIRECTIONS: Answer the following questions directly, briefly, and succinctly.

1. What is usually done with exhaust steam from an engine?
2. How many wires would you use in running a 220-volt line for 110-volt consumption?
3. What is the top of a boiler called in which steam is collected and then conducted to a steam engine?
4. What is the instrument called which measures the density or specific gravity of a solution?
5. What is a steam engine called in which steam is exhausted directly into the air?
6. What is the difference between a water-tube and a fire-tube boiler?
7. On what do the brushes ride in a generator producing direct current?
8. What heat unit is used for grading coal?
9. What is the opening in a cylinder face for the passage of exhaust steam called?
10. What provision is made on the receiver of an ammonia system for excessive pressure?

2 (#3)

KEY (CORRECT ANSWERS)

1. Heating
   Processing

2. Three

3. Dome (drum) (chest) (head) (header)

4. Hydrometer

5. Noncondensing

6. Water-tube has water in tubes
   Fire-tube has fire in tubes

7. Commutator

8. British Thermal Unit (B.T.U.)

9. Exhaust port (port)

10. Relief (safety) (pressure) valve

READING COMPREHENSION
UNDERSTANDING AND INTERPRETING WRITTEN MATERIAL
EXAMINATION SECTION
TEST 1

DIRECTIONS: Each question or incomplete statement is followed by several suggested answers or completions. Select the one that BEST answers the question or completes the statement. *PRINT THE LETTER OF THE CORRECT ANSWER IN THE SPACE AT THE RIGHT.*

Questions 1-2.

DIRECTIONS: Questions 1 and 2 are to be answered SOLELY on the basis of the following paragraph.

When fixing an upper sash cord, you must also remove the lower sash. To do this, the parting strip between the sash must be removed. Now remove the cover from the weight box channel, cut off the cord as before, and pull it over the pulleys. Pull your new cord over the pulleys and down into the channel where it may be fastened to the weight. The cord for an upper sash is cut off 1" or 2" below the pulley with the weight resting on the floor of the pocket and the cord held taut. These measurements allow for slight stretching of the cord. When the cord is cut to length, it can be pulled up over the pulley and tied with a single common knot in the end to fit into the socket in the sash groove. If the knot protrudes beyond the face of the sash, tap it gently to flatten. In this way, it will not become frayed from constant rubbing against the groove.

1. When repairing the upper sash cord, the FIRST thing to do is to
    A. remove the lower sash
    B. cut the existing sash cord
    C. remove the parting strip
    D. measure the length of new cord necessary

1._____

2. According to the above paragraph, the rope may become frayed if the
    A. pulley is too small   B. knot sticks out
    C. cord is too long   D. weight is too heavy

2._____

Questions 3-4.

DIRECTIONS: Questions 3 and 4 are to be answered SOLELY on the basis of the following paragraph.

Repeated burning of the same area should be avoided. Burning should not be done on impervious, shallow, unstable, or highly erodible soils, or on steep slopes—especially in areas subject to heavy rains or rapid snowmelt. When existing vegetation is likely to be killed or seriously weakened by the fire, measures should be taken to assure prompt revegetation of the burned area. Burns should be limited to relatively small proportions of a watershed unit so that the stream channels will be able to carry any increased flows with a minimum of damage.

3. According to the above paragraph, planned burning should be limited to small areas of the watershed because
    A. the fire can be better controlled
    B. existing vegetation will be less likely to be killed
    C. plants will grow quicker in small areas
    D. there will be less likelihood of damaging floods

3._____

4. According to the above paragraph, burning USUALLY should be done on soils that
    A. readily absorb moisture
    B. have been burnt before
    C. exist as a thin layer over rock
    D. can be flooded by nearby streams

4._____

Questions 5-11.

DIRECTIONS: Questions 5 through 11 are to be answered SOLELY on the basis of the following paragraph.

FUSE INFORMATION

Badly bent or distorted fuse clips cannot be permitted. Sometimes, the distortion or bending is so slight that it escapes notice, yet it may be the cause for fuse failures through the heat that is developed by the poor contact. Occasionally, the proper spring tension of the fuse clips has been destroyed by overheating from loose wire connections to the clips. Proper contact surfaces must be maintained to avoid faulty operation of the fuse. Maintenance men should remove oxides that form on the copper and brass contacts, check the clip pressure, and make sure that contact surfaces are not deformed or bent in any way. When removing oxides, use a well-worn file and remove only the oxide film. Do not use sandpaper or emery cloth as hard particles may come off and become embedded in the contact surfaces. All wire connections to the fuse holders should be carefully inspected to see that they are tight.

5. Fuse failure because of poor clip contact or loose connections is due to the resulting
    A. excessive voltage   B. increased current
    C. lowered resistance   D. heating effect

5._____

6. Oxides should be removed from fuse contacts by using
    A. a dull file   B. emery cloth
    C. fine sandpaper   D. a sharp file

6._____

7. One result of loose wire connections at the terminal of a fuse clip is stated in the above paragraph to be
    A. loss of tension in the wire
    B. welding of the fuse to the clip
    C. distortion of the clip
    D. loss of tension of the clip

7._____

8. Simple reasoning will show that the oxide film referred to is undesirable CHIEFLY because it
   A. looks dull
   B. makes removal of the fuse difficult
   C. weakens the clips
   D. introduces undesirable resistance

8._____

9. Fuse clips that are bent very slightly
   A. should be replaced with new clips
   B. should be carefully filed
   C. may result in blowing of the fuse
   D. may prevent the fuse from blowing

9._____

10. From the fuse information paragraph, it would be reasonable to conclude that fuse clips
    A. are difficult to maintain
    B. must be given proper maintenance
    C. require more attention than other electrical equipment
    D. are unreliable

10._____

11. A safe practical way of checking the tightness of the wire connection to the fuse clips of a live 120-volt lighting circuit is to
    A. feel the connection with your hand to see if it is warm
    B. try tightening with an insulated screwdriver or socket wrench
    C. see if the circuit works
    D. measure the resistance with an ohmmeter

11._____

Questions 12-13.

DIRECTIONS: Questions 12 through 13 are to be answered SOLELY on the basis of the following paragraph.

For cast iron pipe lines, the middle ring or sleeve shall have *beveled* ends and shall be high quality cast iron. The middle ring shall have a minimum wall thickness of 3/8" for pipe up to 8", 7/16" for pipe 10" to 30", and 1/2" for pipe over 30", nominal diameter. Minimum length of middle ring shall be 5" for pipe up to 10", 6" for pipe 10" to 30", and 10" for pipe 30" nominal diameter and larger. The middle ring shall not have a center pipe stop, unless otherwise specified.

12. As used in the above paragraph, the word *beveled* means MOST NEARLY
    A. straight   B. slanted   C. curved   D. rounded

12._____

13. In accordance with the above paragraph, the middle ring of a 24" nominal diameter pipe would have a minimum wall thickness and length of _____ thick and _____ long.
    A. 3/8"; 5:
    B. 3/8"; 6"
    C. 7/16"; 6"
    D. 1/2"; 6"

13._____

Questions 14-17.

DIRECTIONS: Questions 14 through 17 are to be answered SOLELY on the basis of the following paragraph.

Operators spotting loads with long booms and working around men need the smooth, easy operation and positive control of uniform pressure swing clutches. There are no jerks or grabs with these large disc-type clutches because there is always even pressure over the entire clutch lining surface. In the conventional band-type swing clutch, the pressure varies between dead and live ends of the band. The uniform pressure swing clutch has excellent provision for heat dissipation. The driving elements, which are always rotating, have a great number of fins cast in them. This gives them an impeller or blower action for cooling, resulting in longer life and freedom from frequent adjustment.

14. According to the above paragraph, it may be said that conventional band-type swing clutches have
    A. even pressure on the clutch lining
    B. larger contact area
    C. smaller contact area
    D. uneven pressure on the clutch lining

14.____

15. According to the above paragraph, machines equipped with uniform pressure swing clutches will
    A. give better service under all conditions
    B. require no clutch adjustment
    C. give positive control of hoist
    D. provide better control of swing

15.____

16. According to the above paragraph, it may be said that the rotation of the driving elements of the uniform pressure swing clutch is ALWAYS
    A. continuous   B. constant
    C. varying   D. uncertain

16.____

17. According to the above paragraph, freedom from frequent adjustment is due to the
    A. operator's smooth, easy operation
    B. positive control of the clutch
    C. cooling effect of the rotating fins
    D. larger contact area of the bigger clutch

17.____

Questions 18-22.

DIRECTIONS: Questions 18 through 22 are to be answered SOLELY on the basis of the following paragraphs.

Exhaust valve clearance adjustment on diesel engines is very important for proper operation of the engine. Insufficient clearance between the exhaust valve stem and the rocker arm causes a loss of compression and, after a while, burning of the valves and valve seat inserts. On the other hand, too much valve clearance will result in noisy operation of the engine.

Exhaust valves that are maintained in good operating condition will result in efficient combustion in the engine. Valve seats must be true and unpitted, and valve stems must work smoothly within the valve guides. Long valve life will result from proper maintenance and operation of the engine.

Engine operating temperatures should be maintained between 160°F and 185°F. Low operating temperatures result in incomplete combustion and the deposit of fuel lacquers on valves.

18. According to the above paragraphs, too much valve clearance will cause the engine to operate
    A. slowly   B. noisily   C. smoothly   D. cold

    18._____

19. On the basis of the information given in the above paragraphs, operating temperatures of a diesel engine should be between
    A. 125°F and 130°F   B. 140°F and 150°F
    C. 160°F and 185°F   D. 190°F and 205°F

    19._____

20. According to the above paragraphs, the deposit of fuel lacquers on valves is caused by
    A. high operating temperatures
    B. insufficient valve clearance
    C. low operating temperatures
    D. efficient combustion

    20._____

21. According to the above paragraphs, for efficient operation of the engine, valve seats must
    A. have sufficient clearance
    B. be true and unpitted
    C. operate at low temperatures
    D. be adjusted regularly

    21._____

22. According to the above paragraphs, a loss of compression is due to insufficient clearance between the exhaust valve stem and the
    A. rocker arm   B. valve seat
    C. valve seat inserts   D. valve guides

    22._____

Questions 23-25.

DIRECTIONS: Questions 23 through 25 are to be answered SOLELY on the basis of the following excerpt:

A SPECIFICATION FOR ELECTRIC WORK FOR THE CITY

Breakers shall be equipped with magnetic blowout coils...Handles of breakers shall be trip-free...Breakers shall be designed to carry 100% of trip rating continuously; to have inverse time delay tripping above 100% of trip rating...

23. According to the above paragraph, the breaker shall have provision for
    A. resetting   B. arc quenching
    C. adjusting trip time   D. adjusting trip rating

    23._____

24. According to the above paragraph, the breaker
    A. shall trip easily at exactly 100% of trip rating
    B. shall trip instantly at a little more than 100% of trip rating
    C. should be constructed so that it shall not be possible to prevent it from opening on overload or short circuit by holding the handle in the ON position
    D. shall not trip prematurely at 100% of trip rating

    24._____

25. According to the above paragraph, the breaker shall trip 25._____
    A. instantaneously as soon as 100% of trip rating is reached
    B. instantaneously as soon as 100% of trip rating is exceeded
    C. more quickly the greater the current, once 100% of trip rating is exceeded
    D. after a predetermined fixed time lapse, once 100% of trip rating is reached

---

KEY (CORRECT ANSWERS)

1.	C		11.	B
2.	B		12.	B
3.	D		13.	C
4.	A		14.	D
5.	D		15.	D
6.	A		16.	A
7.	D		17.	C
8.	D		18.	B
9.	C		19.	C
10.	B		20.	C

21.	B
22.	A
23.	B
24.	C
25.	C

TEST 2

DIRECTIONS: Each question or incomplete statement is followed by several suggested answers or completions. Select the one that BEST answers the question or completes the statement. *PRINT THE LETTER OF THE CORRECT ANSWER IN THE SPACE AT THE RIGHT.*

Questions 1-4.

DIRECTIONS: Questions 1 through 4 are to be answered SOLELY on the basis of the following paragraph.

A low pressure hot water boiler shall include a relief valve or valves of a capacity such that with the heat generating equipment operating at maximum, the pressure cannot rise more than 20 percent above the maximum allowable working pressure (set pressure) if that is 30 p.s.i. gage or less, nor more than 10 percent if it is more than 30 p.s.i. gage. The difference between the set pressure and the pressure at which the valve is relieving is known as *over-pressure or accumulation.* If the steam relieving capacity in pounds per hour is calculated, it shall be determined by dividing by 1,000 the maximum BTU output at the boiler nozzle obtainable from the heat generating equipment, or by multiplying the square feet of heating surface by five.

1. In accordance with the above paragraph, the capacity of a relief valve should be computed on the basis of
    A. size of boiler
    B. maximum rated capacity of generating equipment
    C. average output of the generating equipment
    D. minimum capacity of generating equipment

1._____

2. In accordance with the above paragraph, with a set pressure of 30 p.s.i. gage, the overpressure should not be more than _____ p.s.i.
    A. 3   B. 6   C. 33   D. 36

2._____

3. In accordance with the above paragraph, a relief valve should start relieving at a pressure equal to the
    A. set pressure
    B. over pressure
    C. over pressure minus set pressure
    D. set pressure plus over pressure

3._____

4. In accordance with the above paragraph, the steam relieving capacity can be computed by
    A. *multiplying* the maximum BTU output by 5
    B. *dividing* the pounds of steam per hour by 1,000
    C. *dividing* the maximum BTU output by the square feet of heating surface
    D. *dividing* the maximum BTU output by 1,000

4._____

Questions 5-8.

DIRECTIONS: Questions 5 through 8 are to be answered SOLELY on the basis of the following paragraph.

Air conditioning units requiring a minimum rate of flow of water in excess of one-half (1/2) gallon per minute shall be metered. Air conditioning equipment with a refrigeration unit which has a definite rate of capacity in tons or fractions thereof, the charge will be at the rate of $30 per annum per ton capacity from the date installed to the date when the supply is metered. Such units, when equipped with an approved water-conserving device, shall be charged at the rate of $4.50 per annum per ton capacity from the date installed to the date when the supply is metered.

5. A man who was in the market for air conditioning equipment was considering three different units. Unit 1 required a flow of 28 gallons of water per hour; Unit 2 required 30 gallons of water per hour; Unit 3 required 32 gallons of water per hour. The man asked the salesman which units would require the installation of a water meter. According to the above passage, the salesman SHOULD answer:
    A. All three units require meters
    B. Units 2 and 3 require meters
    C. Unit 3 only requires a meter
    D. None of the units require a meter

6. Suppose that air conditioning equipment with a refrigeration unit of 10 tons was put in operation on October 1; and in the following year on July 1, a meter was installed. According to the above passage, the charge for this period would be _____ the annual rate.
    A. twice   B. equal to
    C. three-fourths   D. one-fourth

7. The charge for air conditioning equipment which has no refrigeration unit
    A. is $30 per year
    B. is $25.50 per year
    C. is $4.50 per year
    D. cannot be determined from the above passage

8. The charge for air conditioning equipment with a seven-ton refrigeration unit equipped with an approved water-conserving device
    A. is $4.50 per year
    B. is $25.50 per year
    C. is $31.50 per year
    D. cannot be determined from the above passage

Questions 9-14.

DIRECTIONS: Questions 9 through 14 are to be answered SOLELY on the basis of the following paragraph.

The city makes unremitting efforts to keep the water free from pollution. An inspectional force under a sanitary expert is engaged in patrolling the watersheds to see that the department's sanitary regulations are observed. Samples taken daily from various points in the water supply system are examined and analyzed at the three laboratories maintained by the department. All water before delivery to the distribution mains is treated with chlorine to destroy bacteria. In addition, some water is aerated to free it from gases and, in some cases, from microscopic organisms. Generally, microscopic organisms which develop in the reservoirs and at times impart an unpleasant taste and odor to the water, though in no sense harmful to health, are destroyed by treatment with copper sulfate and by chlorine dosage. None of the supplies is filtered, but the quality of the water supplied by the city is excellent for all purposes, and it is clear and wholesome.

9. According to the above paragraph, microscopic organisms are removed from the water supplied to the city by means of
    A. chlorine alone
    B. chlorine, aeration, and filtration
    C. chlorine, aeration, filtration, and sampling
    D. copper sulfate, chlorine, and aeration

9._____

10. Microscopic organisms in the water supply GENERALLY are
    A. a health menace
    B. impossible to detect
    C. not harmful to health
    D. not destroyed in the water

10._____

11. The MAIN function of the inspectional force, as described in the above paragraph, is to
    A. take samples of water for analysis
    B. enforce sanitary regulations
    C. add chlorine to the water supply
    D. inspect water-use meters

11._____

12. According to the above paragraph, chlorine is added to water before entering the
    A. watersheds
    B. reservoirs
    C. distribution mains
    D. run-off areas

12._____

13. Of the following suggested headings or titles for the above paragraph, the one that BEST tells what the paragraph is about is
    A. QUALITY OF WATER
    B. CHLORINATION OF WATER
    C. TESTING OF WATER
    D. BACTERIA IN WATER

13._____

14. The MOST likely reason for taking samples of water for examination and analysis from various points in the water supply system is:
    A. The testing points are convenient to the department's laboratories
    B. Water from one part of the system may be made undrinkable by a local condition
    C. The samples can be distributed equally among the three laboratories
    D. The hardness or softness of water varies from place to place

14._____

Questions 15-17.

DIRECTIONS: Questions 15 through 17 are to be answered SOLELY on the basis of the following paragraph.

A building measuring 200' x 100' at the street is set back 20' on all sides at the 15th floor, and an additional 10' on all sides at the 30th floor. The building is 35 stories high.

15. The floor area of the 16th floor is MOST NEARLY _____ sq. ft.
    A. 20,000   B. 14,400   C. 9,600   D. 7,500

16. The floor area of the 35th floor is MOST NEARLY _____ sq. ft.
    A. 20,000   B. 13,900   C. 7,500   D. 5,600

17. The floor area of the 16th floor, compared to the floor area of the 2nd floor, is MOST NEARLY _____ as much.
    A. three-fourths (3/4)   B. two-thirds (2/3)
    C. one-half (1/2)   D. four-tenths (4/10)

Question 18.

DIRECTIONS: Question 18 is to be answered SOLELY on the basis of the following paragraph.

Experience has shown that, in general, a result of the installation of meters on services not previously metered is to reduce the amount of water consumed, but is not necessarily to reduce the peak load on plumbing systems. The permissible head loss through meters at their rated maximum flow is 20 p.s.i. The installation of a meter may therefore appreciably lower the pressures available in fixtures on a plumbing system.

18. According to the above paragraph, a water meter may
    A. limit the flow in the plumbing system of 20 p.s.i.
    B. reduce the peak load on the plumbing system
    C. increase the overall amount of water consumed
    D. reduce the pressure in the plumbing system

Question 19.

DIRECTIONS: Question 19 is to be answered SOLELY on the basis of the following paragraph.

Spring comes without trumpets to a city. The asphalt is a wilderness that does not quicken overnight; winds blow gritty with cinders instead of merry with the smells of earth and fertilizer. Women wear their gardens on their hats. But spring is a season in the city, and it has its own harbingers, constant as daffodils. Shop windows change their colors, people walk more slowly on the streets, what one can see of the sky has a bluer tone. Pulitzer prizes awake and sing and matinee tickets go-a-begging. But gayer than any of these are the carousels, which are already in sheltered places, beginning to turn with the sound of springtime itself. They are the earliest and the truest and the oldest of all the urban signs.

19. In the passage above, the word *harbingers* means
    A. storms   B. truths   C. virtues   D. forerunners

Questions 20-22.

DIRECTIONS: Questions 20 through 22 are to be answered SOLELY on the basis of the following paragraph.

Gas heaters include manually operated, automatic, and instantaneous heaters. Some heaters are equipped with a thermostat which controls the fuel supply so that when the water falls below a predetermined temperature, the fuel is automatically turned on. In some types, the hot-water storage tank is well-insulated to economize the use of fuel. Instantaneous heaters are arranged so that the opening of a faucet on the hot-water pipe will increase the flow of fuel, which is ignited by a continuously burning pilot light to heat the water to from 120° to 130°F. The possibility that the pilot light will die out offers a source of danger in the use of automatic appliances which depend on a pilot light. Gas and oil heaters are dangerous, and they should be designed to prevent the accumulation, in a confined space within the heater, of a large volume of an explosive mixture.

20. According to the above passage, the opening of a hot-water faucet on a hot-water pipe connected to an instantaneous hot-water heater will the pilot light.
    A. *increase* the temperature of
    B. *increase* the flow of fuel to
    C. *decrease* the flow of fuel to
    D. *have a marked effect* on

20._____

21. According to the above passage, the fuel is automatically turned on in a heater equipped with a thermostat whenever
    A. the water temperature drops below 120°F
    B. the pilot light is lit
    C. the water temperature drops below some predetermined temperature
    D. a hot water supply is opened

21._____

22. According to the above passage, some hot-water storage tanks are well-insulated to
    A. accelerate the burning of the fuel
    B. maintain the water temperature between 120° and 130°F
    C. prevent the pilot light from being extinguished
    D. minimize the expenditure of fuel

22._____

Question 23.

DIRECTIONS: Question 23 is to be answered SOLELY on the basis of the following paragraph.

Breakage of the piston under high-speed operation has been the commonest fault of disc piston meters. Various techniques are adopted to prevent this, such as *throttling* the meter, cutting away the edge of the piston, or reinforcing it, but these are simply makeshifts.

23. As used in the above paragraph, the word *throttling* means MOST NEARLY
    A. enlarging   B. choking
    C. harnessing   D. dismantling

23._____

Questions 24-25.

DIRECTIONS: Questions 24 and 25 are to be answered SOLELY on the basis of the following paragraph.

One of the most common and objectionable difficulties occurring in a drainage system is trap seal loss. This failure can be attributed directly to inadequate ventilation of the trap and the subsequent negative and positive pressures which occur. A trap seal may be lost either by siphonage and/or back pressure. Loss of the trap seal by siphonage is the result of a negative pressure in the drainage system. The seal content of the trap is forced by siphonage into the waste piping of the drainage system through exertion of atmospheric pressure on the fixture side of the trap seal.

24. According to the above paragraph, a positive pressure is a direct result of
    A. siphonage
    B. unbalanced trap seal
    C. poor ventilation
    D. atmospheric pressure

25. According to the above paragraph, the water in the trap is forced into the drain pipe by
    A. atmospheric pressure
    B. back pressure
    C. negative pressure
    D. back pressure on fixture side of seal

KEY (CORRECT ANSWERS)

1.	B	11.	B
2.	B	12.	C
3.	D	13.	A
4.	D	14.	B
5.	C	15.	C
6.	C	16.	D
7.	D	17.	C
8.	C	18.	D
9.	D	19.	B
10.	C	20.	B

21. C
22. D
23. B
24. C
25. A

ARITHMETICAL REASONING
EXAMINATION SECTION
TEST 1

DIRECTIONS: Each question or incomplete statement is followed by several suggested answers or completions. Select the one that BEST answers the question or completes the statement. *PRINT THE LETTER OF THE CORRECT ANSWER IN THE SPACE AT THE RIGHT.*

1.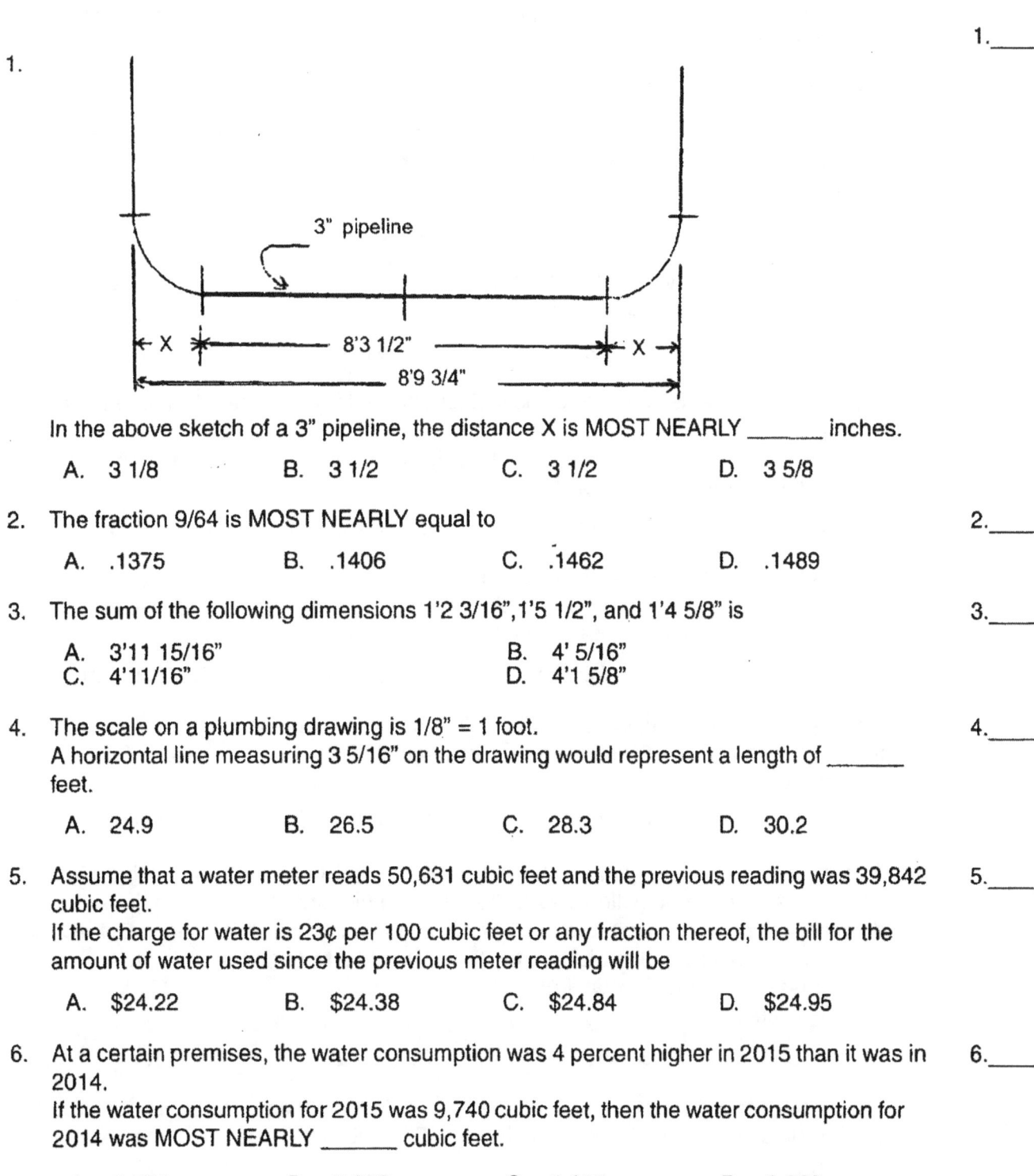

   In the above sketch of a 3" pipeline, the distance X is MOST NEARLY _____ inches.

   A. 3 1/8   B. 3 1/2   C. 3 1/2   D. 3 5/8

2. The fraction 9/64 is MOST NEARLY equal to

   A. .1375   B. .1406   C. .1462   D. .1489

3. The sum of the following dimensions 1'2 3/16", 1'5 1/2", and 1'4 5/8" is

   A. 3'11 15/16"   B. 4' 5/16"
   C. 4'11/16"   D. 4'1 5/8"

4. The scale on a plumbing drawing is 1/8" = 1 foot.
   A horizontal line measuring 3 5/16" on the drawing would represent a length of _____ feet.

   A. 24.9   B. 26.5   C. 28.3   D. 30.2

5. Assume that a water meter reads 50,631 cubic feet and the previous reading was 39,842 cubic feet.
   If the charge for water is 23¢ per 100 cubic feet or any fraction thereof, the bill for the amount of water used since the previous meter reading will be

   A. $24.22   B. $24.38   C. $24.84   D. $24.95

6. At a certain premises, the water consumption was 4 percent higher in 2015 than it was in 2014.
   If the water consumption for 2015 was 9,740 cubic feet, then the water consumption for 2014 was MOST NEARLY _____ cubic feet.

   A. 9,320   B. 9,350   C. 9,365   D. 9,390

69

7. A pump delivers water at a constant rate of 40 gallons per minute.
   If there are 7.5 gallons to a cubic foot of water, the time it will take to fill a tank 6 feet x 5 feet x 4 feet is MOST NEARLY _____ minutes.

   A. 15   B. 22.5   C. 28.5   D. 30

8. The total weight, in pounds, of three lengths of 3" cast-iron pipe 7'6" long, weighing 14.5 pounds per foot, and four lengths of 4" cast-iron pipe each 5'0" long, weighing 13.0 pounds per foot, is MOST NEARLY

   A. 540   B. 585   C. 600   D. 665

9. The water pressure at the bottom of a column of water 34 feet high is 14.7 lbs./sq.in.
   The water pressure in lbs./sq.in. at the bottom of the column of water 12 feet high is MOST NEARLY

   A. 3   B. 5   C. 7   D. 9

10. The number of cubic yards of earth that would be removed when digging a trench 8 feet wide x 9 feet deep x 63 feet long is

    A. 56   B. 168   C. 314   D. 504

11. On test, a meter registered one cubic foot for each 1 1/3 cubic feet of water that passed through it.
    If the meter had a reading of 1,200 cubic feet, we may conclude that the CORRECT amount should be _____ cubic feet.

    A. 800   B. 900   C. 1,500   D. 1,600

12. A water use meter reads 87,463 cubic feet.
    If the previous reading was 17,377 cubic feet and the rate charged is 15 cents per 100 cubic feet, the bill for water use during this period is about

    A. $45.00   B. $65.00   C. $85.00   D. $105.00

13. Under proper conditions, the one of the following groups of pipes that gives the same flow in gals/min as one 6" diameter pipe is (neglect friction) _____ pipes of _____ diameter each.

    A. 3; 3"   B. 4; 3"   C. 2; 4"   D. 3; 4"

14. A roof tank is used to furnish the domestic water supply to a ten story building. This tank has a capacity of 5,900 gallons. At 10:00 A.M. one morning, the tank is half full.
    If water is being used at the rate of 50 gals/min, the pump which is used to fill the tank has a rated capacity of 90 gals/min, the time it would take to fill the tank under these conditions is MOST NEARLY _____ hour(s), _____ minutes.

    A. 2; 8   B. 1; 14   C. 2; 32   D. 1; 2

15. The number of gallons of water contained in a cylindrical swimming pool 8 feet in diameter and filled to a depth of 3 feet 6 inches is MOST NEARLY (assume 7.5 gallons = 1 cubic foot)

    A. 30   B. 225   C. 1,320   D. 3,000

16. The charge for metered water is 52 1/2 cents per hundred cubic feet, with a minimum charge of $21 per annum. Of the following, the SMALLEST water usage in hundred cubic feet that would result in a charge GREATER than the minimum is

    A. 39   B. 40   C. 41   D. 42

17. The annual frontage rent on a one-story building 40 ft. in length is $735.00. For each additional story, $52.50 per annum is added to the frontage rent. For demolition, the charge for wetting down is 3/8 of the annual frontage charge.
    The charge for wetting down a building six stories in height, with a 40 ft. frontage, is MOST NEARLY

    A. $369   B. $371   C. $372   D. $374

18. If the drawing of a piping layout is made to a scale of 1/4" equals one foot, then a 7'9" length of piping would be represented by a scaled length on the drawing of APPROXIMATELY _____ inches.

    A. 2   B. 7 3/4   C. 23 1/4   D. 31

19. A plumbing sketch is drawn to a scale of eighth-size. A line measuring 3" on the sketch would be equivalent to _____ feet.

    A. 2   B. 6   C. 12   D. 24

20. If 500 feet of pipe weighs 800 lbs., the number of pounds that 120 feet will weigh is MOST NEARLY

    A. 190   B. 210   C. 230   D. 240

21. If a trench is excavated 3'0" wide by 5'6" deep and 50 feet long, the total number of cubic yards of earth removed is MOST NEARLY

    A. 30   B. 90   C. 150   D. 825

22. Assume that a plumber earns $86,500 per year.
    If eighteen percent of his pay is deducted for taxes and social security, his net weekly pay will be APPROXIMATELY

    A. $1,326   B. $1,365   C. $1,436   D. $1,457.50

23. Assume that a plumbing installation is made up of the following fixtures and groups of fixtures: 12 bathroom groups each containing one W.C., one lavatory, and one bathtub with shower; 12 bathroom groups each containing one W.C., one lavatory, one bathtub, and one shower stall; 24 combination kitchen fixtures; 4 floor drains; 6 slop sinks without flushing rim; and 2 shower stalls (or shower bath).
    The total number of fixtures for the above plumbing installation is MOST NEARLY

    A. 60   B. 95   C. 120   D. 210

24. A triangular opening in a wall forms a 30-60 degree right triangle.
    If the longest side measures 12'0", then the shortest side will measure

    A. 3'0"   B. 4'0"   C. 6'0"   D. 8'0"

25. You are directed to cut 4 pieces of pipe, one each of the following length: 2'6 1/4", 3'9 3/8", 4'7 5/8", and 5'8 7/8".
 The total length of these 4 pieces is

 A. 15'7 1/4" B. 15'9 3/8" C. 16'5 7/8" D. 16'8 1/8"

KEY (CORRECT ANSWERS)

1. A 11. D
2. B 12. D
3. B 13. B
4. B 14. B
5. C 15. C

6. C 16. C
7. B 17. D
8. B 18. A
9. B 19. A
10. B 20. A

21. A
22. B
23. C
24. C
25. D

SOLUTIONS TO PROBLEMS

1. 8'3 1/2" + x + x = 8'9 3/4" Then, 2x = 6 1/4", so x = 3 1/8"

2. 9/64 = .140625 = .1406

3. 1'2 3/16" + 1'5 1/2" +1'4 5/8" = 3'11 21/16" = 4'5/16"

4. 3 5/16" ÷ 1/8" =53/16 x 8/1 = 26.5. Then, (26.5)(1 ft.) = 26.5 feet

5. 50,631 - 39,842 = 10,789; 10,789 ÷ 100 = 107.89
   Since the cost is .23 per 100 cubic feet or any fraction thereof, the cost will be
   (.23)(107) + .23 = $24.84

6. 9740 ÷ 1.04 = 9365 cu.ft.

7. 40 ÷ 7.5 = 5 1/3 cu.ft. of water per minute. The volume = (6)(5)(4) = 120 cu.ft. Thus, the number of minutes needed to fill the tank is 120 ÷ 5 1/3 = 22.5

8. 3" pipe: 3 x 7'6" = 22 1/2' x 14.5 lbs. = 326.25
   4" pipe: 4 x 5' = 20' x 13 lbs. = 260
   326.25 + 260 = 586.25 (most nearly 585)

9. Let x = pressure. Then, 34/12 = 14.7/x. So, 34x = 176.4
   Solving, x ≈ 5 lbs./sq.in.

10. (8)(9)(63) = 4536 cu.ft. Since 1 cu.yd. = 27 cu.ft., 4536 cu.ft. is equivalent to 168 cu.yds.

11. Let x = correct amount. Then, $\frac{1}{1200} = \frac{1\frac{1}{3}}{x}$. Solving, x = 1600

12. 87,463 - 17,377 = 70,086; and 70,086 ÷ 100 = 700.86 ≈ 700 Then, (700)(.15) = $105.00

13. Cross-sectional area of a 6" diameter pipe = (π)(3")^2 = 9π sq. in. Note that the combined cross-sectional areas of four 3" diameter pipes = (4)(π)(1.5")^2 = 9π sq. in.

14. 90 - 50 = 40 gals/min. Then, 2950 ÷ 40 = 73.75 min. ≈ 1 hr. 14 min.

15. Volume = (π)(4)^2(3 1/2) = 56π cu.ft. Then, (56π)(7.5) = 1320 gals.

16. For 4100 cu.ft., the charge of (.525)(41) = $21,525 > $21

17. Rent = $73,500 + (5)($52.50) = $997,50. For demolition, the charge = (3/8)($997.50) $374

18. (1/4")(7.75) = 2"

19. (3")(8) = 24" = 2 ft.

6 (#1)

20. Let x = weight. Then, 500/800 = 120/x . Solving, x = 192 190 lbs.

21. (3')(5 1/2')(50') = 825 cu.ft. Then, 825 ÷ 27 ≈ 30 cu.yds.

22. Net pay = (.82)($86,500) = $70,930/yr. Weekly pay = $70,930 ÷ 52 ≈ $1365

23. (12x3) + (12x4) +24+4+6+2= 120

24. The shortest side = (1/2)(hypotenuse) = (1/2)(12') = 6'

25. 2'6 1/4" + 3'9 3/8" + 4'7 5/8" + 5'8 7/8 " = 14'30 17/8" = 16'8 1/8"

TEST 2

DIRECTIONS: Each question or incomplete statement is followed by several suggested answers or completions. Select the one that BEST answers the question or completes the statement. *PRINT THE LETTER OF THE CORRECT ANSWER IN THE SPACE AT THE RIGHT.*

1. The sum of the following pipe lengths, 15 5/8", 8 3/4", 30 5/16" and 20 1/2", is 1.____

    A. 77 1/8"   B. 76 3/16"   C. 75 3/16"   D. 74 5/16"

2. If the outside diameter of a pipe is 6 inches and the wall thickness is 1/2 inch, the inside area of this pipe, in square inches, is MOST NEARLY 2.____

    A. 15.7   B. 17.3   C. 19.6   D. 23.8

3. Three lengths of pipe 1'10", 3'2 1/2", and 5'7 1/2", respectively, are to be cut from a pipe 14'0" long.
Allowing 1/8" for each pipe cut, the length of pipe remaining is 3.____

    A. 3'1 1/8"   B. 3'2 1/2"   C. 3'3 1/4"   D. 3'3 5/8"

4. According to the building code, the MAXIMUM permitted surface temperature of combustible construction materials located near heating equipment is 76.5°C. (°F=(°Cx9/5)+32)
Maximum temperature Fahrenheit is MOST NEARLY 4.____

    A. 170° F   B. 195° F   C. 210° F   D. 220° F

5. A pump discharges 7.5 gals/minutes.
In 2.5 hours the pump will discharge _____ gallons. 5.____

    A. 1125   B. 1875   C. 1950   D. 2200

6. A pipe with an outside diameter of 4" has a circumference of MOST NEARLY _____ inches. 6.____

    A. 8.05   B. 9.81   C. 12.57   D. 14.92

7. A piping sketch is drawn to a scale of 1/8" = 1 foot.
A vertical steam line measuring 3 1/2" on the sketch would have an ACTUAL length of _____ feet. 7.____

    A. 16   B. 22   C. 24   D. 28

8. A pipe having an inside diameter of 3.48 inches and a wall thickness of .18 inches will have an outside diameter of _____ inches. 8.____

    A. 3.84   B. 3.64   C. 3.57   D. 3.51

9. A rectangular steel bar having a volume of 30 cubic inches, a width of 2 inches, and a height of 3 inches will have a length of _____ inches. 9.____

    A. 12   B. 10   C. 8   D. 5

10. A pipe weighs 20.4 pounds per foot of length.
The total weight of eight pieces of this pipe with each piece 20 feet in length is MOST NEARLY _____ pounds. 10.____

    A. 460   B. 1,680   C. 2,420   D. 3,260

11. Assume that four pieces of pipe measuring 2'1 1/4", 4'2 3/4", 5'1 9/16", and 6'3 5/8", respectively, are cut with a saw from a pipe 20"0" long.
    Allowing 1/16" waste for each cut, the length of the remaining pipe is

    A. 2'1 9/16"   B. 2'2 9/16"   C. 2'4 13/16"   D. 2'8 9/16"

12. If one cubic inch of steel weighs 0.28 pounds, the weight, in pounds, of a steel bar 1/2" x 6" x 2'0" long is MOST NEARLY

    A. 11   B. 16   C. 20   D. 24

13. If the circumference of a circle is equal to 31.416 inches, then its diameter, in inches, is equal to MOST NEARLY

    A. 8   B. 9   C. 10   D. 13

14. Assume that a steam fitter's helper receives a salary of $171.36 a day for 250 days is considered a full work year. If taxes, social security, hospitalization, and pension deducted from his salary amounts to 16 percent of his gross pay, then his net yearly salary will be MOST NEARLY

    A. $31,788   B. $35,982   C. $41,982   D. $42,840

15. If the outside diameter of a pipe is 14 inches and the wall thickness is 1/2 inch, then the inside area of the pipe, in square inches, is MOST NEARLY

    A. 125   B. 133   C. 143   D. 154

16. A steam leak in a pipe line allows steam to escape at a rate of 50,000 pounds each month.
    Assuming that the cost of steam is $2.50 per 1,000 pounds, the TOTAL cost of wasted steam from this leak for a 12-month period would amount to

    A. $125   B. $300   C. $1,500   D. $3,000

17. If 250 feet of 4" pipe weighs 400 pounds, the weight of this pipe per linear foot is _____ pounds.

    A. 1.25   B. 1.50   C. 1.60   D. 1.75

18. A set of heating plan drawings is drawn to a scale of 1/4" = 1 foot.
    If a length of pipe measures 4 5/8" on the drawing, the ACTUAL length of the pipe, in feet, is

    A. 16.3   B. 16.8   C. 17.5   D. 18.5

19. The TOTAL length of four pieces of pipe whose lengths are 3'4 1/2", 2'1 5/16", 4'9 3/8", and 2'3 1/4", respectively, is

    A. 11'5 7/16"   B. 11'6 7/16"
    C. 12'5 7/16"   D. 12'6 7/16"

20. Assume that a pipe trench is 3 feet wide, 3 feet deep, and 300 feet long.
    If the unit cost of excavating the trench is $120 per cubic yard, the TOTAL cost of excavating the trench is

    A. $1,200   B. $12,000   C. $27,000   D. $36,000

21. The TOTAL length of four pieces of 1 1/2" galvanized steel pipe whose lengths are 7 ft. + 3 1/2 inches, 4 ft. + 2 1/4 inches, 6 ft. + 7 inches, and 8 ft. +5 1/8 inches is   21.____

    A. 26 feet + 5 7/8 inches
    B. 25 ft. + 6 7/8 inches
    C. 25 feet + 4 1/4 inches
    D. 25 ft. + 3 3/8 inches

22. A swimming pool is 25' wide by 75' long and has an average depth of 5'. 1 cubic foot contains 7.5 gallons of water. The capacity, when filled to the overflow, is _____ gallons.   22.____

    A. 9,375   B. 65,625   C. 69,005   D. 70,312

23. The sum of 3 1/4, 5 1/8, 2 1/2, and 3 3/8 is   23.____

    A. 14   B. 14 1/8   C. 14 1/4   D. 14 3/8

24. Assume that it takes 6 men 8 days to do a particular job. If you have only 4 men available to do this job and they all work at the same speed, then the number of days it would take to complete the job would be   24.____

    A. 11   B. 12   C. 13   D. 14

25. The total length of four pieces of 2" O.D. pipe, whose lengths are 7'3 1/2", 4'2 3/16", 5'7 5/16", and 8'5 7/8", respectively, is MOST NEARLY   25.____

    A. 24'6 3/4"
    B. 24'7 15/16"
    C. 25'5 13/16"
    D. 25'6 7/8"

KEY (CORRECT ANSWERS)

1.	C	11.	B
2.	C	12.	C
3.	D	13.	C
4.	A	14.	B
5.	A	15.	B
6.	C	16.	C
7.	D	17.	C
8.	A	18.	D
9.	D	19.	D
10.	D	20.	B

21. A
22. D
23. C
24. B
25. D

SOLUTIONS TO PROBLEMS

1. 15 5/8" + 8 3/4" + 30 5/16" + 20 1/2" = 73 35/16" = 75 3/16"

2. Inside diameter = 6" - 1/2" - 1/2" = 5". Area = $(\pi)(5/2")^2 \approx$ 19.6 sq. in.

3. Pipe remaining = 14' - 1'10" - 3'2 1/2" - 5'7 1/2" - (3)(1/8") = 3'3 5/8"

4. 76.5 x 9/5 = 137.7 + 32 = 169.7

5. 7.5 x 150 = 1125

6. Radius = 2" Circumference = $(2\pi)(2") \approx$ 12.57"

7. 3 1/2" 1/8" = (7/2)(8/1) = 28 Then, (28)(1 ft.) = 28 feet

8. Outside diameter = 3.48" + .18" + .18" = 3.84"

9. 30 = (2)(3)(length). So, length = 5"

10. Total weight = (20.4)(8)(20) $\approx$ 3260 lbs.

11. 20' - 2'1 1/4" - 4'2 3/4" - 5'1 9/16" - 6'3 5/8" - (4)(1/16") = 2'2 9/16"

12. Weight = (.28)(1/2")(6")(24") = 20.16 $\approx$ 20 lbs.

13. Diameter = 31.416" ÷ $\pi \approx$ 10"

14. His net pay for 250 days = (.84)($171.36)(250) = $35,985.60 $\approx$ $35,928 (from answer key)

15. Inside diameter = 14" - 1/2" - 1/2" = 13". Area = $(\pi)(13/2")^2 \approx$ 133 sq.in

16. (50,000 lbs.)(12) = 600,000 lbs. per year. The cost would be ($2.50)(600) = $1500

17. 400 ÷ 250 = 1.60 pounds per linear foot

18. 4 5/8" ÷ 1/4" = 37/8 . 4/1 = 18.5 Then, (18.5)(1 ft.) = 18.5 feet

19. 3'4 1/2" + 2'1 5/16" + 4'9 3/8" + 2'3 1/4" = 11'17 23/16" = 12'6 7/16"

20. (3')(3')(300') = 2700 cu.ft., which is 2700 ÷ 27 = 100 cu.yds. Total cost = ($120)(100) = $12,000

21. 7'3 1/2" + 4'2 1/4" + 6'7" + 8'5 1/8" = 25'17 7/8" = 26'5 7/8"

22. (25)(75)(5) = 9375 cu.ft. Then, (9375)(7.5) $\approx$ 70,312 gals.

23. 3 1/4 + 5 1/8 + 2 1/2 + 3 3/8 = 13 10/8 = 14 1/4

24. (6)(8) = 48 man-days. Then, 48 ÷ 4 = 12 days

25. 7'3 1/2" + 4'2 3/16" + 5'7 5/16" + 8'5 7/8" = 24'17 30/16" = 25'6 7/8"

TEST 3

DIRECTIONS: Each question or incomplete statement is followed by several suggested answers or completions. Select the one that BEST answers the question or completes the statement. *PRINT THE LETTER OF THE CORRECT ANSWER IN THE SPACE AT THE RIGHT.*

1. The time required to pump 2,500 gallons of water out of a sump at the rate of 12 1/2 gallons per minutes would be _____ hour(s) _____ minutes. 1._____

    A. 1; 40   B. 2; 30   C. 3; 20   D. 6; 40

2. Copper tubing which has an inside diameter of 1 1/16" and a wall thickness of .095" has an outside diameter which is MOST NEARLY _____ inches. 2._____

    A. 1 5/32   B. 1 3/16   C. 1 7/32   D. 1 1/4

3. Assume that 90 gallons per minute flow through a certain 3-inch pipe which is tapped into a street main. 3._____
    The amount of water which would flow through a 1-inch pipe tapped into the same street main is MOST NEARLY _____ gpm.

    A. 90   B. 45   C. 30   D. 10

4. The weight of a 6 foot length of 8-inch pipe which weighs 24.70 pounds per foot is _____ lbs. 4._____

    A. 148.2   B. 176.8   C. 197.6   D. 212.4

5. If a 4-inch pipe is directly coupled to a 2-inch pipe and 16 gallons per minute are flowing through the 4-inch pipe, then the flow through the 2-inch pipe will be _____ gallons per minute. 5._____

    A. 4   B. 8   C. 16   D. 32

6. If the water pressure at the bottom of a column of water 34 feet high is 14.7 pounds per square inch, the water pressure at the bottom of a column of water 18 feet high is MOST NEARLY _____ pounds per square inch. 6._____

    A. 8.0   B. 7.8   C. 7.6   D. 7.4

7. If there are 7 1/2 gallons in a cubic foot of water and if water flows from a hose at a constant rate of 4 gallons per minute, the time it should take to COMPLETELY fill a tank of 1,600 cubic feet capacity with water from that hose is _____ hours. 7._____

    A. 300   B. 150   C. 100   D. 50

8. Each of a group of fifteen water meter readers read an average of 62 water meters a day in a certain 5-day work week. A total of 5,115 meters are read by this group the following week. 8._____
    The TOTAL number of meters read in the second week as compared to the first week shows a

    A. 10% increase   B. 15% increase
    C. 20% increase   D. 5% decrease

9. A certain water consumer used 5% more water in 1994 than he did in 1993. If his water consumption for 1994 was 8,375 cubic feet, the amount of water he consumed in 1993 was MOST NEARLY _____ cubic feet.

   A. 9,014   B. 8,816   C. 7,976   D. 6,776

10. Assume that a water meter reads 40,175 cubic feet and that the previous reading was 29,186 cubic feet.
    If the charge for water is 92 cents per 100 cubic feet or any fraction thereof, the bill for the amount of water used since the previous meter reading should be

    A. $100.28   B. $101.04   C. $101.08   D. $101.20

11. A leaking faucet caused a loss of 216 cubic feet of water in a 30-day month. If there are 7.5 gallons in a cubic foot of water, then the AVERAGE loss of water per hour for that month was _____ gallons.

    A. 2 1/4   B. 2 1/8   C. 2   D. 1 3/4

12. The fraction which is equal to .375 is

    A. 3/16   B. 5/32   C. 3/8   D. 5/12

13. A square backyard swimming pool, each side of which is 10 feet long, is filled to a depth of 3 1/2 feet.
    If there are 7 1/2 gallons in a cubic foot of water, the number of gallons of water in the pool is MOST NEARLY _____ gallons.

    A. 46.7   B. 100   C. 2,625   D. 3,500

14. When 1 5/8, 3 3/4, 6 1/3, and 9 1/2 are added, the resulting sum is

    A. 21 1/8   B. 21 1/6   C. 21 5/24   D. 21 1/4

15. When 946 1/2 is subtracted from 1,035 1/4, the result is

    A. 87 1/4   B. 87 3/4   C. 88 1/4   D. 88 3/4

16. When 39 is multiplied by 697, the result is

    A. 8,364   B. 26,283   C. 27,183   D. 28,003

17. When 16.074 is divided by .045, the result is

    A. 3.6   B. 35.7   C. 357.2   D. 3,572

18. To dig a trench 3'0" wide, 50'0" long, and 5'6" deep, the total number of cubic yards of earth to be removed is MOST NEARLY

    A. 30   B. 90   C. 140   D. 825

19. The TOTAL length of four pieces of 2" pipe, whose lengths are 7'3 1/2", 4'2 3/16", 5'7 5/16", and 8'5 7/8", respectively, is

    A. 24'6 3/4"   B. 24'7 15/16"
    C. 25'5 13/16"   D. 25'6 7/8"

3 (#3)

20. A hot water line made of copper has a straight horizontal run of 150 feet and, when installed, is at a temperature of 45° F. In use, its temperature rises to 190° F.
If the coefficient of expansion for copper is 0.0000095" per foot per degree F, the TOTAL expansion, in inches, in the run of pipe is given by the product of 150 multiplied by 0.0000095 by

   A. 145
   B. 145 x 12
   C. 145 divided by 12
   D. 145 x 12 x 12

21. A water storage tank measures 5' long, 4' wide, and 6' deep and is filled to the 5 1/2' mark with water.
If one cubic foot of water weighs 62 pounds, the number of pounds of water required to COMPLETELY fill the tank is

   A. 7,440   B. 6,200   C. 1,240   D. 620

22. Assume that a pipe worker earns $83,125.00 per year.
If seventeen percent of his pay is deducted for taxes, social security, and pension, his net weekly pay will be APPROXIMATELY

   A. $1598.50   B. $1504.00   C. $1453.00   D. $1325.00

23. If eighteen feet of 4" cast iron pipe weighs approximately 390 pounds, the weight of this pipe per lineal foot will be MOST NEARLY _____ lbs.

   A. 19   B. 22   C. 23   D. 25

24. If it takes 3 men 11 days to dig a trench, the number of days it will take 5 men to dig the same trench, assuming all work is done at the same rate of speed, is MOST NEARLY

   A. 6 1/2   B. 7 3/4   C. 8 1/4   D. 8 3/4

25. If a trench is dug 6'0" deep, 2'6" wide, and 8'0" long, the area of the opening, in square feet, is MOST NEARLY

   A. 48   B. 32   C. 20   D. 15

KEY (CORRECT ANSWERS)

1. C
2. D
3. D
4. A
5. B

6. B
7. D
8. A
9. C
10. D

11. A
12. C
13. C
14. C
15. D

16. C
17. C
18. A
19. D
20. A

21. D
22. D
23. B
24. A
25. C

SOLUTIONS TO PROBLEMS

1. 2500 ÷ 12 1/2 = 200 min. = 3 hrs. 20 min.

2. 1 1/16" + .095" + .095" = 1.0625 + .095 + .095 = 1.2525" ≈ 1 1/4"

3. Cross-sectional areas for a 3-inch pipe and a 1-inch pipe are $(\pi)(1.5)^2$ and $(\pi)(.5)^2$ = 2.25π and $.25\pi$, respectively. Let x = amount of water flowing through the 1-inch pipe. Then, $\frac{90}{x} = \frac{2.25\pi}{.25\pi}$. Solving, x = 10 gals/min

4. (24.70)(6) = 148.2 lbs.

5. $\frac{4" \text{ pipe}}{16 \text{ gallons}} = \frac{2" \text{ pipe}}{x \text{ gallons}}$, 4x = 32, x = 8

6. Let x = pressure. Then, 34/18 = 14.7/x. Solving, x ≈ 7.8

7. (1600)(7.5) = 12,000 gallons. Then, 12,000 ÷ 4 = 3000 min. = 50 hours

8. (15)(62)(5) = 4650. Then, (5115-4650)/4650 = 10% increase

9. 8375 ÷ 1.05 ≈ 7976 cu.ft.

10. 40,175 - 29,186 = 10,989 cu.ft. Then, 10,989 100 = 109.89. Since .92 is charged for each 100 cu.ft. or fraction thereof, total cost = (.92)(110) = $101.20

11. (216)(7.5) = 1620 gallons. In 30 days, there are 720 hours. Thus, the average water loss per hour = 1620 ÷ 720 = 2 1/4 gallons.

12. .375 = 375/1000 = 3/8

13. Volume = (10)(10)(3 1/2) = 350 cu.ft. Then, (350)(7 1/2) = 2625 gallons

14. 1 5/8 + 3 3/4 + 6 1/3 + 9 1/2 = 19 53/24 = 21 5/24

15. 1035 1/4 - 946 1/2 = 88 3/4

16. (39)(697) = 27,183

17. 16.074 .045 = 357.2

18. (3')(50')(5 1/2') = 825 cu.ft. ≈ 30 cu.yds., since 1 cu.yd. = 27 cu.ft.

19. 7'3 1/2" + 4'2 3/16" + 5'7 5/16" + 8'5 7/8" = 24'17 30/16" = 25'6 7/8"

20. Total expansion = (150)(.0000095)(145)

21. Number of pounds needed = (5)(4)(6-5 1/2)(62) = 620

6 (#3)

22. Net annual pay = ($83,125)(.83) ≈ $69000. Then, the net weekly pay = $69000 ÷ 52 ≈ $1325 (actually about $1327)

23. 390 lbs. ÷ 18 = 21.6 lbs. per linear foot

24. (3)(11) = 33 man-days. Then, 33 ÷ 5 = 6.6 ≈ 6 1/2 days

25. Area = (8')(2 1/2') = 20 sq.ft.

BASIC FUNDAMENTALS OF BOILERS

TABLE OF CONTENTS

		Page
I.	NATURE	1
II.	CLASSIFICATION	2
	A. Location of Fire and Water Spaces	2
	B. Size of Tubes	2
	C. Type of Circulation	2
	D. Type of Superheat	3
III.	TERMINOLOGY	3
	A. Fire Room and Boiler Room	4
	B. Boiler Emergency Station	4
	C. Boiler Full-Power Capacity	4
	D. Boiler Overload Capacity	4
	E. Superheater Outlet Pressure	4
	F. Steam Drum Pressure	4
	G. Design Pressure	4
	H. Operating Pressure	4
	I. Boiler Efficiency	4
	J. Fire Room Efficiency	4
	K. Total Heating Surface	5
	L. Generating Surface	5
	M. Superheater Surface	5
	N. Economizer Surface	5
	O. Steaming Hours	5

BASIC FUNDAMENTALS OF BOILERS

I. NATURE

The boiler is the source or high-temperature region of the thermos-dynamic cycle. The steam that is generated in the boiler is led to the turbines, where its thermal energy is converted into mechanical energy (work) which drives the unit and provides power for vital services.

In essence, a boiler is merely a container in which water can be boiled and steam generated. A tea kettle on a stove is basically a boiler, although a rather inefficient one. Note that the steam is generated in one vessel and superheated in another, since it is impossible to raise the temperature of the steam above the temperature of the boiling water as long as the two are in contact with each other.

In designing a boiler which must produce a large amount of steam, it is obviously necessary to find some means of providing a larger amount of heat-transfer surface than could be provided by a vessel shaped like a tea kettle. In most modern boilers, the steam generating surface consists of hundreds and hundreds of tubes, which provide a maximum amount of heat-transfer surface in a relatively small space. As a rule, the tubes communicate with a steam drum at the top of a boiler and with water drums and headers at the bottom of the boiler. The tubes and part of the drums are enclosed in an insulated capsule which has space inside it for the furnace. A boiler appears to be a fairly complicated piece of equipment when it is considered with all its fittings, piping, and accessories; it may be helpful, therefore, to remember that the basic components of a saturated-steam boiler are merely the tubes, the drums, and headers, and the furnace.

Practically all boilers used in propulsion are designed to produce both saturated steam and superheated steam. To our basic boiler, therefore, we must now add another component: the superheater. The superheater on most boilers consist of headers, usually located at the back of the boiler, and a number of superheater tubes which communicate with the headers. Saturated steam from the steam drum is led through the superheater; since the steam is now no longer in contact with the water from which it was generated, the steam becomes superheated as additional heat is supplied. In some boilers, there is a separate superheater furnace; in others, the superheater tubes project into the same furnace that is used for the generation of saturated steam.

Some question may arise concerning the need for both saturated steam and superheated steam. Saturated steam is used for operating most steam-driven auxiliary machinery; reciprocating machinery, in particular, requires saturated steam for the lubrication of the moving parts of the steam end. Superheated steam is used almost exclusively for the propulsion turbines. There is more available energy in superheated steam than in saturated steam at the same pressure; and the use of higher temperatures vastly increases the efficiency of the propulsion cycle since, as we have seen, the efficiency of a heat engine is dependent upon the absolute temperature at the source (boiler) and the absolute temperature at the receiver (condenser). In some instances, the gain in efficiency resulting from the use of superheated steam may be as much as 15 percent for 200 degrees of superheat. This increase in efficiency is particularly important because it allows substantial savings in fuel consumption and in space and weight requirements. A further advantage in using superheated steam for propulsion machinery is that it causes relatively little erosion since it is free of moisture

II. CLASSIFICATION

Boilers may be classified in a number of different ways, according to various design features. Most commonly, they are classified and described in terms of (1) the relative location of the fire and water spaces, (2) the size of the tubes, (3) the type of circulation, and (4) the type of superheat. Some knowledge of these methods of classification will be useful in understanding the design and construction of modern boilers.

A. Location of Fire and Water Spaces

First of all, boilers are classified according to the relative location of their fire and water spaces. By this classification, all boilers may be divided into two groups: *fire-tube boilers* and *water-tube boilers*. In *fire-tube boilers*, the gases of combustion flow through the tubes and thereby heat the surrounding water. In *water-tube boilers*, the water flows through the tubes and is heated by the gases of combustion that fill the furnace.

B. Size of Tubes

Water-tube boilers are further classified according to the size of the tubes. Boilers having tubes 2 inches or more in diameter are called *large-tube boilers*. Boilers having tubes less than 2 inches in diameter are called *small-tube* or *express-type boilers*.

C. Type of Circulation

Water-tube boilers are also classified as *natural circulation boilers* or as *force circulation boilers*, depending upon the way in which the water circulates within the boiler.

Natural circulation boilers are those in which the circulation of water depends upon the difference in density between an ascending mixture of hot water and steam and a descending body of relatively cool and steam-free water. Natural circulation may be of two types, free or accelerated.

In this type of boiler, the generating tubes are installed at a slight angle of inclination which allows the lighter hot water and steam to rise while the cooler (and heavier) water descends.

Installing the generating tubes at a greater angle of inclination increases the rate of water circulation. Hence, boilers in which the tubes slope more steeply are said to have accelerated natural circulation.

Most modern boilers are designed for accelerated natural circulation. In such boilers, large tubes (3 or more inches in diameter) are installed between the steam drum and the water drums. These tubes, called *downcomers*, are located outside the furnace and away from the heat of combustion, thereby serving as pathways for the downward flow of relatively cool water. When a sufficient number of downcomers are installed, all small tubes can be generating tubes, carrying steam and water upward; and all downward flow can be carried by the downcomer. The size and number of downcomers installed varies from one type of boiler to another.

Forced circulation boilers are, as their name implies, quite different in design from the boilers that utilize natural circulation. Instead of depending upon differences in density between the hotter and the cooler water, forced circulation boilers use pumps to force the water through the various boiler circuits. Forced circulation boilers are relatively new, but they have some very definite advantages which will probably lead to their increased use in the future.

D. Type of Superheat

Practically all boilers are equipped with superheaters. With respect to the superheater installation, boilers are classified as having either controlled superheat or uncontrolled superheat. In a boiler with *controlled superheat*, the degree of superheat can be changed by regulating the amount of heat supplied to the superheater tube bank, without substantially changing the amount of heat supplied to the generating tubes. This control of superheat is possible because the boiler has two furnaces, one for the saturated side and one for the superheat side. A boiler with *uncontrolled superheat*, on the other hand, has only one furnace; and since the same furnace must be used for heating both the generating tubes and the superheater tubes, the degree of superheat cannot be controlled but varies within a small range as a function of design and firing rate.

Various terms are used to describe these two basic types of superheaters. Where the superheat is controlled, the superheater is often referred to as an *integral, separately fired superheat*, and the boiler as a whole is called a *superheat control boiler*. Where the superheat is not controlled, the superheater may be called an *integral, not separately fired superheater*, or it may be referred to as a *no control,* or *uncontrolled superheater*, and the boiler as a whole is called a *no control* or *uncontrolled superheat boiler*. The term *integral* is used to indicate that the superheater is installed as a part of the boiler unit. Practically all superheaters on modern boilers are integral with the boilers.

On both controlled and uncontrolled superheat boilers, the superheater tubes are protected from radiant heat by generation tubes that are called *water screen tubes*. The water screen tubes absorb the intense radiant heat of the furnace, and the superheater tubes are heated by convection currents rather than by direct radiation. Hence, the superheaters are sometimes called *convection-type superheaters*.

Some older types of superheat control boilers had *radiant-type superheaters*—that is, the superheater tubes were not screened by water tubes but were exposed directly to the radiant heat of the furnace. However, this type of superheater is relatively uncommon at the present time and will, therefore, not be further discussed.

III. TERMINOLOGY

In order to ensure uniform use of terms, there has been established a number of standard terms and definitions pertaining to boilers. Some of the more important of these definitions are given below.

A. Fire Room and Boiler Room: A compartment which contains boilers and the station for operating them is called a *fire room*. A compartment which contains boilers which does not contain the station for operating them is called a *boiler room*.

B. Boiler Emergency Station: This term is used to designate a station which is so located that, in the event of trouble, one may proceed with minimum delay to any fire room, boiler operating station, or boiler room.

C. Boiler Full-Power Capacity: The total quantity of steam required to develop contract shaft horsepower of the vessel, divided by the number of boilers installed, gives boiler full-power capacity. The quantity of steam is given in pounds of water evaporated per hour. Full-power capacity is indicated in the manufacturer's technical manual for each boiler.

D. Boiler Overload Capacity: Boiler overload capacity is specified in the design of the boiler. It is given in terms of steaming rate or firing rate, depending upon the individual installation. Boiler overload capacity is usually 120 percent of boiler full-power capacity.

E. Superheater Outlet Pressure: This is the actual steam pressure at the superheater outlet.

F. Steam Drum Pressure: This is the pressure in the steam drum. Steam drum pressure is specified in the design of a boiler and is given in the manufacturer's technical manual for each boiler. Steam drum pressure is the pressure which must be carried in the boiler steam drum in order to obtain the required pressure at the turbine throttles, when steaming at full-power capacity. Ordinarily, the designed steam drum pressure is carried for all steaming conditions.

G. Design Pressure: Design pressure is the pressure specified by the boiler manufacturer as a criterion for boiler design. It is usually 103 percent of steam drum pressure.

H. Operating Pressure: Operating pressure is the pressure at the final outlet from a boiler, after steam has passed through all baffles, the dry pipe, the superheater, etc., when the boiler is steaming at full-power capacity. Operating pressure is specified in the design of a boiler and is given in the manufacturer's technical manual. Operating pressure is the same as superheater outlet pressure when the boiler is steaming at full-power capacity; when the boiler is steaming at less than full-power capacity, however, the actual pressure at the superheater outlet will vary from the specified operating pressure provided a constant drum pressure is maintained.

I. Boiler Efficiency: The efficiency of a boiler is the British thermal units per pound of fuel absorbed by the water and steam divided by the British thermal units per pound of fuel fired. In other words, boiler efficiency is output divided by input, or Btu utilized divided by Btu available. Boiler efficiency is expressed as a percentage.

J. Fire Room Efficiency: The boiler efficiency corrected for blower and pump steam consumption is known as fire room efficiency. (This is not the same as boiler plant efficiency or propulsion plant efficiency.)

K. Total Heating Surface: The total heating surface of any steam generating unit consists of that portion of the heat transfer apparatus which is exposed on one side to the gases of combustion and on the other side to the water or steam being heated. Thus, the total heating surface equals the sum of the generating surface, the superheater surface, and the economizer surface. All heating surfaces are measured on the combustion-gas side.

L. Generating Surface: The generating surface is that portion of the total heating surface in which the fluid being heated forms part of the circulating system. The generating surface includes the boiler tube banks, water walls, water screens, and water floors (where installed and not covered by refractory material.)

M. Superheater Surface: The superheater surface is that portion of the total heating surface where the steam is heated after leaving the boiler steam drum.

N. Economizer Surface: The economizer surface is that portion of the total heating surface where the feed water is heated before entering the generating system.

O. Steaming Hours: The term steaming hours includes the time during which the boiler has fires lighted for raising steam and the time during which it is generating steam. Time during which fires are not lighted is not included in steaming hours.